One Woman's Journey to a Better Life

J. R. LUCY

Order this book online at www.trafford.com
or email orders@trafford.com

Most Trafford titles are also available at major online book retailers.

Printed in the United States of America.

ISBN: 978-1-4907-0986-4 (sc)
ISBN: 978-1-4907-0987-1 (hc)
ISBN: 978-1-4907-0988-8 (e)

Library of Congress Control Number: 2013913610

Trafford rev. 07/31/2013

www.trafford.com

North America & international
toll-free: 1 888 232 4444 (USA & Canada)
fax: 812 355 4082

Dedication

Thank you to all who encouraged me to write this book

Life with the Mad Lady

I lived in a household consisting of a physically and emotionally absent father and a younger brother who spent most of his time in the backyard with his beloved dog or rabbit, and as such it was rather lonely for me while I contended with my mother. My father was a very quiet man and worked as a fruit carter and then a milkman in the early years of my life. We didn't see much of him because of his work schedule, and when he was at home, he spent most of his time out in the garage building or fixing things. He was smart enough to stay out of Mum's way for as long as possible, and he spent quite a few hours out in his boat, fishing. He knew she didn't like the water, so there was no danger of her wanting to go with him. She didn't particularly like eating fish, either, but she would cook enough for us and give the fresh surplus to the neighbours. This was her Lady Bountiful persona coming to the fore.

The house was built just after World War II, and it was a testament to the builder's skills that it survived all the door slamming that went on when Mum was in one of her moods. When she had a tantrum about something, real or imagined, it was up to Dad to get our dinner, and it was usually fried tomatoes with eggs on top, the lid of the pan kept on so that it was all steamy and soggy. To this day I will throw up if that dish is put in front of me, because it brings back too many bad memories; my brother has the same reaction.

I was born in 1944 while Dad was still away at the war, and my brother Charlie arrived in September 1948. He didn't even get a second name because Mum has said on several occasions that she doesn't like boys, so she couldn't be bothered to give him one. At least it doesn't take him long to fill in his name on a form. I suppose it is not much different from Mum telling the nurse to take me away when I was born, because I was too ugly. Oh, sweet motherly love.

I was the child who always had to have the last say. You know the sort—the one who runs away from her parent while still going on about whatever displeased her. When I was small, Mum could outrun me, and I got a hard slap on the closest part of my body, which was usually my head. As I grew taller than she was, she resorted to a vicious tongue lashing with words at which a dockworker would blush. I also knew she would rarely lay into me in public, although one of my aunties related a story about Mum hitting me with a high-heeled shoe when I was small and while we were on holidays together. I think my cousin Neil got it right: he called her the Mad Lady, and he was only a child when he came up with that title.

I did reasonably well at school, and I don't remember getting into much trouble; however, at home it was a whole different story. Mum would lash out and hit me, and I would ask, "What was that for?"

She would answer, "That's just in case you do something." Another mixed message and confusion; nothing was straightforward with her. There was no cause-and-effect equation, just however her mood was on that particular day. She was consistently inconsistent.

There was no chance of Dad standing up to her, and my brother kept his head down and stayed out of her way. He saw the trouble I got into by having my say, and many years later those dynamics remain unchanged. Even when I was sixty-five, she tried to hit me with a potted plant because I dared to defy her.

Over her lifetime, she has managed to alienate almost everybody in the family, my brother and me included. She has fought with my aunties over the most ridiculous things and has not spoken to them for years. My brother and his son won't have anything to do with her, so she sits alone in her big, empty house while Dad is probably happy at his present address.

Temper tantrums, door slamming, not seeing her for two weeks at a time as she hid in her bedroom—these actions were what we thought was a normal way of life when we were young. This was our reality, and we didn't have the opportunity of seeing how other families went about their daily lives. We didn't have relatives or friends come to stay in the house, because Mum actively discouraged this. She had friends amongst the mothers in the neighbourhood, but of course they wouldn't be coming to any sleepovers. They only lived up the street or around the corner, so the danger of them observing anything she preferred to keep secret didn't happen. We also were not encouraged to stay at other people's places.

The only time we spent with our relatives was when we went on holidays as young children, with the families of Dad's middle sister or Mum's brother, but it was usually in two different houses close to each other. They knew how unpredictable Mum was since she was a young woman, and they were not very happy when Dad chose Mum to be his wife.

My brother and I weren't encouraged to stay with either of our grandparents, because Mum didn't get along with her mother-in-law—no surprise there. My mother's mother, whom I called Nevvy, had a house only a few kilometres from us, and over the years several young couples boarded with her. These couples often had children while they were boarding with her and moved on, but she kept in touch with them. My mother didn't approve of this, and although we visited, we didn't stay overnight.

We were well fed and clothed, and we had a comfortable home materially speaking, but there was never a feeling of sanctuary from the big, bad world outside. Our world was actually bad on the inside, because of Mum. I cannot remember my mother or my father putting their arms around me and telling me they loved me, or making me feel they truly cared about me. My first mother-in-law said Mum was a street angel house devil, and how right she was. Mum could be so well behaved when out in public, but as soon as the front door was closed to the outside world, it was a different matter for us kids.

When my mother eventually sought help for her mental illness in the 1960s, her psychiatrist and local doctor medicated her to such an extent that I don't think she really knew what was real and what was not. She had all her medications in two-litre, empty ice cream containers stored in her wardrobe, which I termed her cupboard of multicoloured happiness. She had enough tablets to send the whole community to sleep, and all of it was acquired on prescription, which she was quite happy to dispense to any female neighbour who was having a down day.

My brother rejects medication to this day, even at the risk of heart damage, because of our experiences with Mum's self-medication. I suspect she didn't always get the dosage right. Charlie doesn't even like taking Panadol if he can avoid it. For quite some time, medication for him took the form of several swigs from a bottle with Jack Daniel's on the label; my cure was more the chardonnay variety, a battle I am still waging even now. After all, my maternal grandfather was an alcoholic, so I suspect there is some of that in our genes.

Mum could hold it all together and behave properly while she was taking me to physical culture lessons or ballroom dancing, because it seemed to be important to her that the public saw her as a good mother. For the most part she achieved that aim, because we were well mannered and nicely dressed, and we would seem to be being raised in a happy family. Nobody really saw what went on inside our four walls, because they weren't encouraged to be in the house for any length of time. She only needed to behave in public because once at home, she could do whatever she liked. Dad would never interfere, but then he wasn't home all that often; he had his own issues with her to address.

In a lot of relationships between mothers and daughters, there is love, harmony, support, and trust. Somehow I missed the boat on all of these. I was more scared of my mother than anything else in the world because she was unpredictable, could be violent, and had a vicious tongue. As far as love went, that was never mentioned, let alone exhibited. She would probably say that she showed her love by the nice clothing I wore and the new ballroom dancing dresses I had for every competition, but a hug now and then wouldn't have gone astray.

I have spent the majority of my adult life trying to understand why I was not loved. When Mum and I were out at a shopping centre, for instance, anyone pushing a pram would be her target. She would rush off like a bee to a flower and poke her head into the pram or stroller, sometimes to the amazement of the mother and child. Questions would abound about name, age, and more, and she would tell the bewildered mother how much she loved children. If she loved children so much, why did she treat her own children the way she did? What was it about us, that we were so unlovable that she would lash out for no apparent reason—and with good aim, I might add—but usually only when we were within the four walls of our home?

All my life I have kept people at arm's length, both physically and emotionally, so that I wouldn't be vulnerable to abuse or disappointment. This has led to a lot of difficulties in intimate relationships, and I am nervous if someone wants to get too close. A psychologist once asked me to do an exercise of holding out my hands to the distance I felt safe from harm as he walked towards me. I extended my arms to full length; this told me that was as close as anyone was going to get to me, and they couldn't hit me from that distance. Opening myself up to another human being has always been complex for me, and I have had a lot of counselling in the last twenty years to try to help me understand this difficulty and beat it.

It wasn't until I was in my fifties and seeing a psychologist about depression that I started to understand that my mother had a mental illness. We weren't privy to the diagnosis of it, but we'd had to live with the results.

Please, Mum
21/9/99

Please, Mum, just hold my hand.
The day is hot, and burning is the sand.
I just want you to help me cross over the way.
I promise I won't bother you any more today.

Please, Mum, just put your arms round me.
I long for your touch, and good I'll be.
I'll try to behave for lots more days
And make sure I stay right out of your way.

Please, Mum, don't hit me again.
I'm only little and have nothing to gain.
I don't know the rules you've made for today;
You keep changing them, but never say.

Please, Mum, just hold me tight.
I had a bad dream in the middle of the night.
I miss being cuddled and the softness of touch.
I don't think I really ask for much.

Please, Mum, just listen to me
Without raising your voice and having to scream.
I don't need to be yelled at to understand.
You could just as easily take hold of my hand.

Please, Mum, now that I'm an adult, too,
Are you proud of me, what I've become, and who?
I'm really a nice person if you get to know me.
So please, Mum, can't we now live in harmony?

Doreen's Tick of Approval

My first boyfriend lived on the opposite side of the street, about a hundred yards up the road. He was an older man; I was four and he was six years old. He promised me that he would buy me a two-storey house and a white MG, at that time a very modern sports car. I never did marry him, or live in a two-storey house, or own a white MG, but for all the lack of these things, life has not been too bad.

During my teenage years, Mum gave me such a hard time when I started to go out with a new boyfriend. I wasn't allowed to go on my first date until I was sixteen; I tried to push the envelope a few times and went out secretly, but I always got caught. It really wasn't worth it because when Mum found out, which she always managed to do, I got into real trouble with her. She made my life miserable for as long as she thought my misdemeanour deserved.

My first grown-up boyfriend was a guy I met at work when I was fifteen years old, and he was four years older, which was quite an age gap back in the 1960s. He asked me out about two days before my sixteenth birthday, but Mum said I had to wait until I was sixteen. He took me out for a birthday lunch near where we worked, and I thought it was wonderful. I floated on air for weeks afterwards, and it wasn't long until Peter became a part of our family. He was Catholic and we were Protestant, but when he stayed at our house on weekends, Mum and Dad let him borrow their car to go to church.

We went out together for about two and a half years, and during that time our relationship was purely platonic—which in my virginal state I didn't realise was probably a bit odd. It was more like Peter was my big brother, but back in the 1960s it was too much to contemplate getting pregnant, so hand-holding and some non-threatening kissing was as far as it went. The risk of an unwanted baby that would probably have to be adopted out, and the shame attached to it all, made for very good birth control. It was only "bad" girls who got pregnant, but anyone who was bad was usually smarter than that. The pill, a new invention that spelled freedom from unwanted babies, was only prescribed to those who were about one month from getting married. Doctors wouldn't give it to anyone else who wanted to experiment with their sexuality.

Peter and I split up when I was eighteen; he met someone higher up the social ladder. I eventually got over the hurt, disappointment, and embarrassment of being dumped for someone else. I was footloose and fancy-free, but I didn't know what to do with this freedom and made some awful mistakes with my choice of boyfriends over the next few years.

One boyfriend had a criminal record for stealing. I dated a chef that my mother disliked more than anyone else I went out with, to such a degree that she called him a buck-toothed, pimply faced, skinny Pommy bastard. That romance was doomed to failure from the start because he didn't even get to come in the front door.

My brother learned a lesson by what happened to me, and because he was four years younger, he had a lot of time to learn. When he started taking girls out, he told Mum nothing. She didn't know whether he was with his mates, a new girlfriend, or up to something else. Mum didn't meet her intended daughter-in-law until Charlie and Leanne were actually engaged.

I was made to feel that the normal feelings between a boy and a girl were dirty, and as a result I have never had what I would say was a satisfying sexual relationship. I was very naïve and uninformed. My knowledge of sex consisted of a film at school when I was about twelve, and of Mum handing me a book and instructing me not to ask any questions. I suspect she probably wouldn't have known the answers, anyway. One of my mother's forms of "protection from the opposite sex" for me was to flick the front light on and off if I was sitting in a car at the top of the driveway. If I brought my latest boyfriend into the house, which was not often, then when my mother considered the time was right, she would burst into the kitchen in her dressing gown and with her hair in rollers. That was enough to dampen any young man's ardour, and he would scamper for the front door quickly, rarely to return.

I have never been comfortable with my body, even before the extra kilos of age and cellulite came to stay. There was always the comment from my mother about my big thighs and thick knees, and she happily pointed out that I was built just like Dad's sister, Jane. This was no compliment because Mum couldn't stand his sister, so this was another putdown that she had mastered over the years. I learned to make my own clothes to disguise these figures faults, which were apparently in abundance. But when I look back at photos taken of me between the ages of sixteen and thirty, I was the equivalent of a size ten today—but I always felt like the size of an elephant, and I thought I was ugly. I tried to look as nice as my raw materials would allow me, and I learned early how to do my hair in lots of different ways, using hairpieces for ballroom dancing competitions and always wearing make-up.

In 1965 I finally found someone who my mother accepted as a potential marriage partner for me. I had quite a few boyfriends when I was between the ages of sixteen and twenty that definitely didn't get the Doreen Tick of Approval, now known as DTOA. Dad's opinion was neither sought nor required, because what Mum said was law, and he wasn't going to interfere.

I met David when I was working in a jeweller's store as a secretary. The shop was being refitted, and he was on the team carrying out the work. It wasn't love at first sight, our eyes meeting across the room, or all that romantic nonsense. It was more that I liked the look of him, and he just might fit the DTOA criteria. Most of my previous boyfriends had been tall, dark, and Catholic, and none of them had gotten the DTOA, so I thought I would try for a short, fair Protestant male. Jackpot! The tick for this relationship was waiting in the wings; it was all systems go.

But of course her generosity of spirit couldn't last forever, and after three years of going out together, David and I started to make marriage plans. Well, that really threw a spanner in the works.

My dealings with his mother were only when we went to her place on Sunday night for dinner sometimes, and to a few family outings, so I didn't really know what I was in for. The sacrificial lamb was being led to the slaughter. His mother, Sally, had never been warm and welcoming to me, but I didn't foresee too many problems. Oh, blissful ignorance! David was her youngest child; he had three married sisters, was twenty-seven years old, and lived in her house. He was not exactly a baby, but he was *her* baby, put on earth just to look after her, see to her every need, and never leave her. Then he met me, and his mother's nightmare began. I was engaged to her only son, and she didn't really want me around. She even whinged about having to make a dress to wear to the wedding. David also complained about having to buy a new suit (which he didn't anyway), and when he kneeled down at the altar, the guests saw that he had a hole in his shoe. The enthusiasm level for this wedding was quite low, I would suspect.

One Saturday morning about six weeks before my wedding, Mum decided that she would take an overdose of her multicoloured pills. It should have been a clue when Dad and I were making a cup of tea, and Mum appeared from somewhere, flung open a couple of cupboard doors in the kitchen, slammed them shut, and announced that we wouldn't have to worry about her anymore because she wouldn't be here. Yeah, yeah, yeah—we had heard it all before. There was nothing new here, so we went on about what we were doing and took our cups and some biscuits out on to the back steps to enjoy the morning sunlight. My brother came home from his morning surf and asked us what was going on. Dad and I realised that all was quiet in the house, so we thought we had better investigate this latest tantrum.

Mum had locked herself in the granny flat in the backyard, and Dad had to exert some muscle to break in the door. Mum was a bit out of it, so Dad got her up to walk her around to try to reverse the effect of the pills. At this stage we didn't know what she had taken or how much. I was dispatched to go a few doors away and get the doctor. When he came down, he advised that Mum should go to St John of God Hospital at Burwood, where she could be treated for her overdose and get some help.

For the three weeks that she was in the hospital, I went every day after work to see her, but she wouldn't have anything to do with me. She deliberately turned her face to the wall when I went in her room and wouldn't speak to me. I don't know whether she was blaming me for what she had done, because we never really got to the bottom of what had triggered her suicide attempt in the first place. Communication between us was at its all-time low. Mum came home from the hospital three weeks before my wedding, and we proceeded with having my kitchen tea as though nothing had actually happened. The wedding was getting closer, and there was no discussion at all about why she had tried to end her life. I still don't know and probably never will.

1968: The Wedding

Sally had only met my mother on a few occasions, when I was twenty-four years old and about to marry her only son. She was no keener to have me in the family than I was to be related to her, but David was the common denominator. Some men are thrilled to have two women fight over them, but when it is your mother and your intended wife, the middle is not such a happy place to be.

In 1968 most young couples did not live together before marriage, and they went to the altar pure in white—or maybe some should have worn a cream colour—but living in sin was most definitely frowned upon. I have often thought that if David and I had lived together for even a few months, we would have known that this was a marriage destined for disaster. The dynamics were all wrong: I preferred him to my mother, and he preferred his mother to me.

Because our engagement was so short, I suspect Sally thought I was pregnant, but as time went by that obviously was incorrect. In the lead-up to the wedding, there had been the usual hassles of who wanted what to happen and how things should be done. Everyone had an opinion and took great delight in voicing it, whether or not it was solicited. There were demands made and tears shed, but eventually all the arrangements were finalised for the wedding.

One afternoon, about a month before our wedding, we were sitting on the front veranda of his mother's house at Kennedy Bay. I asked David where we were going to live, and to my absolute surprise he said, "Right here. There is plenty of space, and I won't have to pay rent." My heart almost stopped. I would have to share a house with his mother? Oh, joy. There was no negotiation because he had already decided that was what was going to happen—my opinion was not required.

David and I had some similarities. We were both Australian born, so no culture clash there. We were both Protestant, although his mother thought Methodists were far superior to the Church of England. We were both blond and under five feet five inches. That's about it, I think. Oh yes, and we each had an overbearing and interfering mother. I had left one behind and now lived in the house of the other. Ever heard the saying, "Out of the frying pan and into the fire"? Well, that was my new address.

My mother and I had reasonable dressmaking skills, but my mother-in-law surpassed us in all ways of sewing. I couldn't find the sort of dress that I wanted to wear, so I bought a pattern and altered it accordingly, and Mum and I made it in a few weeks. Due to Sally's eagle eye from her prime position in the front pew of the church, she was able to see that the back of one sleeve was not exactly the same as the other, and she took great delight in telling me so after the ceremony. I really needed to know that right then, I am sure, especially because we were about to stand on the church steps to have our photos taken. No group photos of happy families for this marriage because my mother had decreed that she would not be in a photo with his lot—her words, not mine. That was only one of the difficulties I faced that day, because my mother had no social skills whatsoever. She hasn't managed to accumulate any along the way of her nine-plus decades, either.

To term my mother's behaviour as difficult would be a gross understatement. The dictionary describes difficult as "hard to deal with; troublesome; not easily convinced, pleased or satisfied." She was so much worse than that, and I was getting married for the absolutely wrong reason of wanting to get away from her. Three days out from my wedding, I didn't think I was in love the way I should have been and wanted to call it off, but I allowed myself to be carried along with the tide of wedding preparations because otherwise I would have to stay at home with my mother. In hindsight it seems absolutely ridiculous to go ahead with a wedding to get out of a situation that can no longer be tolerated, but it has been happening since time immemorial, so why should I be any different?

David pointed out that the invitations were out and that we would lose money on the honeymoon. Where were the words "I love you and can't imagine life without you"? Much against my better judgement, I went ahead with the wedding, and when I was standing in front of the minister and saying my vows, all that I could think of was, "I shouldn't be doing this." It should have been glaringly obvious after the minister said, "You may now kiss the bride," to which my new husband replied, "Not on your life, mate," that I should have done an Elvis and left the building.

It was very awkward at the reception following our wedding, and when it came time for the blissful couple (was that us?) to leave, the guests formed a circle. David only said good-bye to his side of the family, and I to mine. After we departed, one of his sisters swooped on the wedding presents and, after reading who they were from, instructed her husband to take all of "their side's" presents back to Sally's place; a neighbour of mine helped Mum and Dad take "my side's" presents back to their place. How ridiculous. We were going to live at Sally's place, but that wasn't taken into account. The wedding presents were opened and displayed in the lounge room for photos. This was the evidence required when it came time for who gave what, and who got what, when dividing up the spoils of the wreckage that results from a failed marriage.

We came home early from our honeymoon because we were bored. The alarm bells should have been going off, but if they were, I ignored them. It was two weeks before Sally made any move to clean out the wardrobe I was supposed to be using. This was just the tip of the iceberg, and it wasn't long before I realised that she viewed me as an interloper.

I was married to her only son, her youngest child, and she didn't really want me there. She definitely called the shots, and it was soon apparent that I had exchanged one tyrannical woman and weak man for another set of the same. David wouldn't stand up to her about anything; what she said was law. I was very familiar with this tactic and had lived with it all my life.

As there was no love lost between David and my mother, she was banned from coming to the house. I hesitate to say "our house" because it was most definitely *her* house, and Sally made no bones about the fact that it was her name on the deed. My mother used to ring up to talk to me, and if Sally answered the phone, she would hold it out in my direction and say, "*She* wants you," in a very nasty voice. No harmony between these families. And so we began our married life.

What young bride (albeit a reluctant one) is going to feel all warm and fuzzy living with a short, fat, grey-haired, interfering old lady who took great delight in reading out the births, deaths, and marriages from the newspaper every evening from the bedroom next door? If there was any sure-fire way to cool the ardour of a new bridegroom, this topped the list. After another night listening to her read the hatches, matches, and dispatches, I told David that I would ram the newspaper down her throat if she kept it up. He got really angry with me and couldn't understand why I was so hot under the collar instead of hot under the nightie.

Life moved on under Sally's rules. Fortunately, I could get away from her all day because I had a full-time job. I was not required to cook meals; Sally would set about getting dinner ready for five o'clock, which was the time they always had dinner—the fact that I didn't get home until six was irrelevant to her. They ate their dinner at the appointed time, and mine rested on top of a slowly simmering saucepan until I arrived. It is hard to love chops that are grilled until they turned up at the edges and peas that lay in a mushy heap with lumpy mashed potatoes that have been kept warm for over an hour.

I could only do our washing on a day Sally wasn't using the clothesline, but there was not really much to put in the machine because she took over washing and ironing David's overalls on her allocated day Monday. They were then ironed by her and placed ready for him to wear. I was not required for this, either. Shopping for food occurred on Saturday morning, when David drove her to the local shops and she chose what we would all eat for the next week. I was not required for this exercise, either, and was never asked if there was something I would like added to the menu.

After living at Sally's place for about three months, David wanted to build a self-contained flat under his mother's house, but we would have to go up through her house to access the outside world. No thanks! He started to do some excavation work, but I didn't want to live in a dungeon under a dragon. However, my opinion was not sought for this project. He needed the money I had saved up to do the work, because he would not consider a bank loan, so I kept my purse strings firmly shut. The work ground to a halt, and many years later it became the garage for the cars of my daughter and son-in-law.

I was twenty-four years old, had been married seven months, was living with a mother-in-law who didn't like me, and had a husband who did what his mother told him. So I decided to have a baby. I didn't bother to mention to David that I was going to go off the pill because I already felt that I was in this marriage by myself. Within two months I was pregnant, and David was not at all keen to tell his mother—maybe she would know that we had been doing "it" in the bedroom right across from hers. I think it must have happened one day when she was out, the television was off, and the papers hadn't been delivered, because our sex life was infrequent and unenthusiastic to say the least.

Sally received the news of my pregnancy with the statement that she had seven grandchildren already, and another one wasn't going to make any difference. It might not matter to her, but it sure was going to be a milestone in my life. I had a good pregnancy, but of course Sally had a lot to say, especially about me wearing a maternity costume and swimming in the pool next door. It was disgraceful, according to her. "In my day, we behaved like ladies." When I left work, I was five months pregnant, so I spent the time until my baby was born walking their corgi, Robbie. It was something to do to get away from spending a day with Sally. It kept me fit, my weight stayed down, and the dog got to have Sally-free time as well. I went to prenatal classes, and when I arrived home after one of these, I was forbidden to talk about it at the table—or anywhere else—because it wasn't "nice". Oh well, I could always talk to the dog and tell him all about it on one of our walks; my husband and mother-in-law weren't interested in this baby I was carrying. My mother, however, was very keen to be a grandmother.

Sally also went on about me booking into a hospital to have my first baby; she had had all four of hers at home. Well, good for her, but I was going where I could be looked after and have medical help if needed. She went on long and loud about how it was inconvenient for David to get to Paddington after work, and when was he supposed to have dinner? I told her he could stay home if it was that much of a problem.

I was to go into hospital on Tuesday, 14 April, to be induced because I was two weeks over my expected due date. On the Sunday before, David had to take his mother out to the cemetery for her to do a bit of polishing of the family plaques and gardening on the graves. It was the designated day for her to go. I was to go into the hospital in forty-eight hours, but nothing stood in the way of what his mother wanted to do. However, to be fair, he did tell me to go next door to their neighbour Jan if anything happened while he was away, because she was a nurse.

When I was packing my bag for the hospital, Sally was appalled that I actually intended to wear a dress and high heels home. In her day (God, I was sick of that phrase), they went home in their dressing gowns, as decent women would. I had just about had enough of her by then, and with my hormones raging, I told her I was not indecent, if that was her inference, and I would be wearing a dress home. I also told her I wouldn't be nursing my new baby on my lap in the car on the way home, because the baby would be secured in a carry basket on the back seat. I received another sniff of disapproval. She sniffed so much I thought she should probably get checked for a nose infection.

Sally noticed that I hadn't put on much weight and told me I would have a skinny baby. Wrong! David had gone home from the hospital at about 8.30 p.m. Tuesday night, and his main concern was whether I could get the baby born that day, 14 April, because it was his father's birthday. I sarcastically said I would see what I could do, as I had been in labour all day. Wasn't it enough that we had married on their wedding anniversary? I had a very healthy 9.7-pound baby girl, whom I named Karen, and she was born at 2.28 a.m. on 15 April 1970. David eventually arrived at about 5.00 a.m. because he had needed his sleep. Good for him!

The new father went down to the nursery to check out what I had produced in his absence and came back to my room with a worried look on his face. He announced that there was something wrong with the baby because she had a red mark on her head. I told him that it was from the forceps delivery and that she was perfectly all right, even though I hadn't seen her since the birth. She was a big baby and was very tired, so she was in the nursery with all the premature babies. She looked totally out of place because she filled the clear, plastic crib from one end to the other. I didn't get to see her until she was nearly twelve hours old, so the bonding didn't get off to a good start.

I had told the obstetrician at one of my prenatal visits that I would need her to ring Mum and tell her when the baby was born, because David had refused to do so. She gave me an odd look but wrote it in the notes anyway. The doctor rang Mum about an hour after Karen's birth to let her know that all was well and that she had a granddaughter. Mum then contacted everyone who was on her "wanting to know list", even though it was 3.30 a.m.

I couldn't breastfeed Karen, another nail in the coffin of failed mothering according to Sally mother. I was on Valium, the drug of choice for post-natal depression in the 1970s, and I was miserable. Mum and David had not managed to bridge the gap in their relationship, and they had devised this ridiculous roster system of visiting me in hospital so they would not be there at the same time. Mum had been instructed that if her rostered visit happened to coincide with the day of the baby's birth, then she was not to go that day.

You will have gathered by now that my mother is not in the habit of following other people's rules. Mum and Dad ignored the instructions from my husband, and they arrived at the hospital for the first visiting session. I was so worried that David would walk in and find them there that I needed something medicinal to calm me down. My first day of motherhood was not going well. Mum and Dad sent flowers, but David threatened to put them in the bin. The flowers from David arrived about four days later, and I duly paid the bill from my own money when I got home from the hospital.

I stayed in hospital for nine days because I really didn't want to go home. I knew I would be subjected to more unasked-for advice, and I would have to learn how to look after this baby without any help from David. My mother couldn't be involved in the day-to-day care, because she wasn't allowed up to the house. I had no sisters or friends who were mothers, so I had to work it out for myself, with many mistakes along the way—which were all pointed out to me by Sally. David had made it quite clear that he was not going to be a hands-on dad, so knowing how to change a nappy or make up a feed was not something he felt he needed to learn how to do. Mum and David were still enemies, so I had to meet Mum in secret at Westfield, or go over to her house when David was at work. Little did I know that when he came home from work, he checked the heat of the car bonnet and the mileage to estimate how long I had been home. He then asked his mother what time I had arrived back. Her answer was usually different than mine, even if only by a few minutes. His mother branded me a liar, along with many other nefarious titles.

As an adult, I had come to realise that I was poorly parented. When my daughter was born, I had no idea what I was supposed to feel, but I knew in my heart there should be something. I used to joke that when the pink cloud of mother love went through the ward, I must have been out in the corridor. I found it very hard to show the love I had for this girl, my only child. I think I concentrated so hard on trying to be a "good mother" that I got lost somewhere; my natural instincts were dampened, and the Valium certainly didn't help. One thing I did know for sure was that this darling daughter of mine would not be terrified of me and what I would do to her if I were in a bad mood.

When Karen was born, my mother exhibited a different side to her personality, and that was one of doting grandmother and spending money like it was going out of fashion. Of course Dad didn't put the brakes on her, or she would have turned on him. I had served my purpose of giving her a grandchild—because she so loved children, you know—and I was the one left out in the driveway with the bags while Mum and Dad swooped on Karen like seagulls to food. I was very conscious of this behaviour when my first grandchild was born, and I always greeted my daughter first and never left her with the bags. I was, and am, a mother first and a grandmother second.

As the months went by and I had to endure days of unasked for advice, things went from impossible to unliveable. I started to pressure David into moving into a place of our own, but he wouldn't hear of it; he couldn't see that there were any problems with the present arrangement. No, of course he didn't, because he was at work all day, and Sally was sweetness and light to him when he arrived home. He had two women looking after him, and it wasn't costing him much money; the fact that his wife was desperately unhappy didn't seem to register.

A big shake-up was required. When Karen was four months old, I left and went to Mum's. It took David three days to find me. How many places did he think I could get to, with a young baby and no money? I have always suspected he only came over to get back his beloved Holden car. When he arrived, he informed me that he thought I had had a breakdown, just like my mother, and I should be put into an institution. There was no way that was going to happen, so I reluctantly went back to his mother's place but begged him to find us somewhere else to live. He told me that if I wanted to move, I could do so—but he wasn't interested. Sally was home most of the week because she had her little routine to follow—washing on Monday, ironing on Tuesday, shopping on Wednesday, cleaning on Thursday, and I forget what Friday was. I couldn't ring real estate agents from *her phone* to find out about what was available, and I felt trapped! I went next door to Jan, and she kindly let me use their phone and relayed the messages from the real estate agents. Sally didn't want me there, I didn't want to be there, and David just wanted peace. I had married a male who wanted peace at any price—that had a familiar ring to it.

When Karen was five months old, I found a converted garage, fully furnished, at Eastlakes that would house us. David was not pleased with my discovery and certainly didn't want to tell his mother he was leaving, but I had made arrangements to move in on the weekend. Well, I might have made arrangements, but David was not being very cooperative. He had to mow the lawns at home and take his mother out to see one of her friends, and he arrived at my mother's place, where I was staying again, at 8.00 p.m. I packed a very sleepy baby into the car with only our immediate requirements, and we set off for our Sally-free home.

The next day was David's first Father's Day, but he chose to spend it with his mother instead, because it was the day to go polishing and floral arranging at the cemetery. I couldn't win. From that day until I moved again, on 26 December, he spent every afternoon at his mother's place doing things for her, or else he was down the road in a phone box calling her.

I went back to Sally's house one morning to collect the rest of my things because I was never going back there. She didn't know I was coming, so I knocked on the door and could hear her footsteps as she thumped through the house. When she opened the door and realised it was me, she was going to shut it in my face, but I stuck my foot in the opening. She had a tape measure draped around her neck, and it was so tempting to cross over the ends and strangle her . . . but I wouldn't look good in jailhouse clothing.

I told her I had come to get the rest of my belongings, so she stood in the doorway of the bedroom while I packed what was mine. She probably thought I was a thief as well as all the other awful character traits I had. I had to leave behind some of Karen's clothes and toys because I couldn't fit everything in the car, and I knew I wouldn't get another chance to collect them.

All the china, glassware, and household items from my glory box (as it was termed in those days) plus the wedding presents were in boxes under Sally's house, and I was unable to retrieve any of them. It took me almost two years to get back what was mine, one box at a time. Of course the wedding presents from "his side" had been stored separately so that there was no chance I would accidentally get any of them. I also left behind the embroidered tablecloths that had been passed on to me by Sally, plus Karen's christening dress and the daisy-pattern pram cover Sally had made. She was welcome to all of them.

When I had transported all my stuff down to the garage, she demanded I give her the door key back, and I told her I didn't want it and wasn't planning on needing it. She could get it from David next time she saw him, probably the same day. It was many years before I set foot in that house again, but she was no longer alive by then.

While I was in this tiny Eastlakes flat—a single-garage, really—I was very depressed. David took the car to a workmate's place every day and left it there to go to work in his mate's car; this tactic was to keep me firmly at home without transport. It didn't work. I put Karen in the pram and walked miles around the streets of Eastlakes. I was probably at my fittest in those months. On some days I met Mum and Dad at an appointed time and went to their place for a few hours. I was so lonely because all my girlfriends were working; I didn't have transport and had very little money; sometimes I had only enough for Karen and me to share an ice cream.

One night in particular, when I was at a very low ebb, I poured a handful of prescription sleeping tablets into my hand and was going to take them. My life was miserable, and I couldn't see how it could possibly improve. At just that moment, Karen cried out in her cot, and I realised that I would be leaving her behind with the people I least wanted to care for her. I poured the pills down the drain, and the crisis was averted. It had really scared me, but I could see how easily a suicide could occur.

I had moved David about twenty kilometres away from his mother, and our marriage wasn't working any better, so I thought that if we moved back nearer to her, he might spend more time with us. I seriously miscalculated on that one—it meant that he could come home from work and go straight to her place, and not waste time and money standing in a hot red phone box making calls. If you can't beat them you don't necessarily have to join them, so I looked around for somewhere closer to his mother. I found a house about a five-minute drive from Sally, at Kogarah, and we had the use of the front half of it. I managed to get David to move our belongings from Eastlakes on 26 December 1970, but by 8 February 1971 this marriage was dead. It was Sally one, Janet nil. His mother was probably glad to get rid of me so that she could have her precious son all to herself again.

I knew when I was beaten and wasn't staying around for the countdown. I left half the dinner set and cutlery and some cooking equipment. I was pretty good with a screwdriver, and I took the cot apart and dismantled the playpen. Then I stacked Karen's clothes and food near the front door. I asked Mum to come over, get Karen, and take her back to her place; I would set about packing up my meagre possessions. I rang a removalist and was out of there.

I was twenty-six years old with a ten-month-old daughter, no car, and very little money. I didn't have a friend back then who would've advised me about having a running-away account. Being short of ready cash was nothing new to me because David had always been stingy with money and doled it out by the dollar. I had to explain what I had spent the previous twenty dollars on that he had given me a week ago. If the explanation was satisfactory, I got the money; if not, I didn't. I don't know what he thought I bought food with, because I certainly wasn't spending the money on myself.

When I went back to live with Mum and Dad in 1971, the first thing I had to do was get a job. This was before the Supporting Parents

Pension, which didn't come in until 1975. I couldn't get a widow's pension, which was the only alternative, because I had left him. He hadn't beaten me and hadn't committed adultery, so I was the party who was financially punished. For four years I had to get by on what I could earn at a casual job. My daughter was too young for me to work full-time, and besides, I wanted to spend time with her and raise her my way—not Mum's way. This is when the wedding gift photos came in handy. Did I want to fight over four glass cake plates? Pity I couldn't have brought into the equation that he preferred to live with his little, old, grey-haired mother than his wife and daughter.

Within a few days of moving to Mum's again, I bought a car with almost a year's registration on it for ninety-five dollars, and Dad and I spray-painted it a lovely sky blue. It wasn't flashy, but it was enough for me to be able to get to and from work, and to take Karen out somewhere throughout the week. I managed to get a casual job the first week after I left David, and it paid me twenty dollars per week. I could only afford to pay six dollars a week board to Mum and Dad, which wasn't nearly enough, but Karen had bad eczema over most of her body, and her ointment was seven dollars per week. I think that at that price, the instruction on the chemist's label, "Use sparingly", was probably superfluous.

I had $1,300 in a fixed deposit account in both David's and my name, which was money I had received when I finished work to have my daughter. After many months of letters between the lawyers, it was decided by the powers that be that half of this money actually belonged to David. He knew it didn't and so did I, but the laws back in the seventies were skewed towards the man. David had money in a bank account with the Commonwealth Bank at Mascot, but I couldn't prove it because his mother held onto the deposit book; it was stashed somewhere in her wardrobe, in an ugly black handbag.

There were no computers back then to electronically search the records, so it was decided that maintenance for Karen at $10 per week did not have to be paid for 65 weeks, which equated to the $650 that was half of the money I had had in the fixed deposit account. It wasn't fair, but it was the law. I applied for an increase in the maintenance when Karen was about ten years old, and it was raised to fifteen dollars per week. It remained at this amount until she left school at seventeen years old.

It was decided that David could see Karen one day each weekend, half of her birthday, half of Christmas day, and half of the school holidays. It is only recently that my daughter told me how much she hated having to spend most of special occasions travelling between her mother and father. It was the law, and I knew that David wouldn't hesitate to contact the police if I refused to let her go out with him. It was so ridiculous that when she had measles, I had to bring her out onto the front veranda at Mum's, wrapped in a rug, so that he could see she was actually ill.

When it was getting to close to the time I could apply for a divorce, I became concerned that David may want to apply for custody of Karen. It was a constant fear for me, and I emotionally held her at arm's length so as not to get too close in case I lost her. This caused me a lot of heartache, and Karen was a very sensitive person even as a little child, so her eczema got worse. She was wrapped in bandages every night from the soles of her feet to her hips, and her arms were covered, too. The bandages were like a bloodbath in the morning because she tried to scratch them off throughout the night.

I made an appointment to see a child psychologist, and after taking a few notes, I was told that the problem lay with me, not Karen, because I was emotionally withdrawn from her. Within a month of my divorce, the eczema started to clear up, and it hasn't been a problem since.

We eventually got divorced when the waiting period of two years elapsed. I got no financial settlement because I couldn't prove what he had stashed away in the ugly black bag, but I did get to have custody of my daughter, and that was a prize in itself. When Karen had been with him on a visit, he had taken photos of her skin and tried to prove that she was neglected. He seriously misjudged this one because his barrister had three children with eczema and didn't take kindly to the inference of neglect. For that tactic, David got to pay fully for Karen's eczema ointment.

Money was a bit short, but I persevered with part-time work so that I could do it one day a week and Saturday morning, and spend the rest of the time with Karen. I could sew and knit, and a neighbour who worked for a fabric company supplied me with samples that were big enough to clothe a young child. I knitted cardigans and jumpers to go with whatever I had sewed, and there was quite a waiting list at the kindergarten for her hand-me-downs.

Without any real reason to think so, I always felt that I would survive and make a life for my daughter and myself.

The Directory of Devious Deeds

I had been divorced from David for a few years, and I felt that it was time to get out a bit and have a social life. I decided to try Parents without Partners (or Pickup with Purpose, as it was also known) because I thought that people with children would understand how it was sometimes difficult to drop everything and go out on a date if a child was sick. I went to a meeting in early October 1974 with another maritally ditched female, and I met James there. In one evening I found out his ex-wife's name, his son's name and age, where he worked, where he lived, and his blood group. Why I needed to be aware of his blood group, I had no idea, but it turned out to be the same as mine. As the years went by, it became the only similarity we had.

We got along really well and liked doing some of the same things. We both liked ballroom dancing, although his counting was a bit less strict than mine, and I often finished up with crushed toes—my fault, of course. He worked in a government job and was a member of the army reserve, so he often spent weekends away "bush bashing," as I called it. I got used to having weekends by myself if David had Karen; I could always find something to do.

When James, or Jim as he was known, and I made arrangements to go out, I always asked Mum first if she could look after Karen, and initially she would agree. As the weeks of our relationship turned into months, she started to show an active dislike towards Jim. She really came into her own and dug deep into her Directory of Devious Deeds to find as many ways as possible to stuff up my burgeoning relationship with him. She hated Jim on sight, mainly because he was male, I suspect, but also because she sensed that this might be the man I would fall in love with and move out, taking her beloved granddaughter with me. She seemed to forget that Karen was my child, not hers. There were many occasions when I would be getting ready to go out, and Karen was fed and bathed. Then Mum would throw a spanner in the works by asking, "And who do you think is going to mind her?" I pointed out that she had agreed, but she would retort, "Well, I have changed my mind." Dad would be sitting close by, saying nothing; he knew which side his bread was buttered on, and it wasn't wise to stand up for me or he would pay for it, one way or another. I had to ring Jim, or wait until he arrived on the doorstep, because there were no mobile phones in 1974. Plans would be changed from going to the movies to eating takeaway Chinese at his place, with Karen wrapped in a rug and asleep on the lounge.

As Karen got older and it was time for her to go to school in 1975, I decided to send her to the Infants, just around the corner. I was working from 9.00 a.m. to 4.00 p.m. at a new job and couldn't pick her up at the end of the school day. Some mornings I dropped her off on my way to work, and other days Dad walked her around to the school. Mum was more than happy to go to the school and collect Karen—most days. When she had one of her off days, she would phone me less than thirty minutes before school finished and inform me that she would not be picking Karen up that day. No explanation. Thank goodness David worked where he could put down tools, leave to collect her, and look after her until I got home. My father, who was home at that time of the day, never went against Mum to support me by collecting his granddaughter. The wrath of Doreen was to be avoided at all costs.

As the months rolled along and I continued to go out with Jim, it was becoming more obvious that I couldn't continue to live with Mum and Dad. I was never quite sure what devious schemes were going on in her head, but one thing I was sure of: it would be something that stuffed up my day. Life was getting to be more and more difficult while living with Mum and Dad, and I thought Mum could see the writing on the wall that I just might move out and live with Jim, which was a very attractive option to me. One Tuesday night in July 1975, Mum and I had another of our arguments, and I couldn't take it anymore. I asked Dad if he would look after Karen for me because she was already in bed, and for maybe the only time in his life, he agreed. I went up to Jim's place, to which I had a key, and rang him at work to tell him he had a temporary boarder. He came straight home from work, and we sat and talked for hours until I had to go home. He wanted me to move in permanently, but I had a daughter to consider; it wasn't just my life I was disrupting, but hers as well. She was only five years old, and I didn't think she would react too well to moving away from her beloved Gramma (as she called Mum) and her Pa. Added into the mix was her father, who wasn't too keen on me living with Jim "in sin".

David came over the next night for a family conference with Mum, Dad, and me; the theme for the evening was "How dare you have a life". All three of them were against the idea that I would move out and live with Jim. David made the mistake of telling me, "You can't have it both ways. You can't live with Jim and take Karen with you."

That was like a red rag to a bull. I replied, "I can and I will—just watch me." I knew it was going to be difficult to integrate Jim, Matthew (Jim's son), Karen, and me into a family unit with the ex-spouses and all that entailed, but I wanted to give it a go. I wasn't going to lose my daughter just because I wanted to move on with my life. I was determined that I was going to have a separate existence from my mother and father; I was thirty years old and divorced, and I was entitled to do that. I realised that it would be a real wrench for Mum and Dad to have Karen move out of what had been her home since February 1971, and whilst I was grateful that I had been allowed to live there, I felt it was unfair that they (really 99 per cent Mum) wanted to continue to dictate the terms of my life.

During the less than supportive negotiations with the three wise monkeys (aka David, Mum, and Dad), I decided that it would appease Mum somewhat if I left Karen with her until Christmas, because I wasn't sure whether it was going to work out with Jim. I needed to find out what our relationship was about before I brought a child to live with us. Besides, Karen didn't like changes in her life and still doesn't.

It has always bothered me why I decided to leave my most precious possession, my child, with my mother, who was less than mentally stable on a good day. It was two decades later that a psychologist helped me work out why I had done that. Apparently it was because I had this imagined bad and good sides of a ledger—the bad side being where I was and the good side being where I was trying to get. I reasoned that if I left my daughter with Mum and therefore appeased her, I would transfer from the bad to the good. I didn't realise that, for her, there was no good side and I would always be on the bad side.

Mum was furious that I was going to live with Jim, and Dad simply went fishing more often. He couldn't stand the arguments; when the going got tough, Dad got going—well away from the shore. The Saturday morning I moved out to go and live with Jim, Mum and I had a tug-of-war on the front lawn over a pair of blankets that belonged on Karen's bed. I wasn't allowed back in the house to get the rest of her things, so whatever was on the front lawn was all that I was going to be able to take with me in my Volkswagen. No problem. I am a person who doesn't like being backed into a corner, so I left Mum with the blankets, which incidentally Karen's father had bought, and went to Jim's place, my new address. On the way there, however, I called into a furniture shop in the nearby shopping centre and ordered a bed and all the other bedding I would need for when Karen came up to stay. They were delivered that afternoon; problem solved.

Between July and December 1975, I kept reinforcing to Karen that at Christmas time she would be coming up to live with Jim and me. She was not the least bit receptive to this idea. I asked her to choose some wallpaper for her room, and she said, "Not my room," so I chose the pattern and applied it to the wall. I got the same response about the carpet, the bedspread, and everything else having to do with moving up with me.

Mum wasn't at all supportive of Karen moving out and put every obstacle she could in my path. When I left work each afternoon, I went over to Mum's to see Karen, and most times she would be out with Dad; these outings could be walking the dog around the golf course behind their house, swimming in a neighbour's pool, and going to the library or shops or anywhere else but home. I sat in the car until she came back, because I knew she had to eventually. I'd see her for an hour or so and then go back to Jim's. I wanted to see her, but my mother was just as keen that I didn't have the opportunity to do so. Persistence is my middle name!

I wanted to have a relationship with a male possibly leading to marriage, although that was not a top priority for me. I had already told Jim that I didn't want to have any more children, because I had a daughter and he had a son. I couldn't see any space in our lives for another child because we would then be "yours, mine, and ours", which might work in television shows but not in real life. This arrangement can be a recipe for a truly dysfunctional family. I had come from a dysfunctional family and didn't need to make another one.

I knew that we would be financially strapped, and he only had a three-bedroom house, which was quite small. Would the new baby share with my daughter, would it take over what was in essence Matthew's room when he came on weekends, or would we have to take out a mortgage on top of the two already in place to fit in a new little person? I would probably have to give up my job, so our finances would be reduced, as well as paying child maintenance for Matthew. Having another child didn't have much going for it as far as I could see, so that idea was removed from the plans. I subsequently had a tubal ligation so that no accidents could happen.

Jim was away with the army reserve at least two weeks twice a year, and often other weekends. Karen went to her father's place on the weekend, and Matthew came to us most weekends. After a while, when Matthew didn't want to be with me any more than I wanted to be with him, mainly because I made him do what he was told, I stated that if Jim wasn't home, then Matthew didn't come over. That well and truly put the cat amongst the pigeons, as the saying goes. Once again, I was supposed to do what made other people happy, irrespective of how it impacted me.

After living together for about eighteen months, Jim wanted to get married, but I was reluctant. I couldn't see any point because we weren't going to have children, and that would be the only reason I would consider another marriage. We argued over this subject quite a lot, and when he was away on one of his army weekends, I put a single bed in the front bedroom and moved our double bed to the back room. I also put a single lounge in the bedroom with me and moved my clothes and things into the wardrobes. It didn't occur to me that Jim might not find this arrangement attractive, because after all it was his house, even though I was living there. When he came home from his army weekend, he was really angry that I had taken it upon myself to reorganise the living spaces and give myself a separate bedroom. I don't know what I was thinking would happen, but when he came home from work the next night, he again expressed his displeasure at having his house turned upside down. I told him that if he wanted to, he could bring his girlfriends in through the back door, I would come in through the front door, and we could use the kitchen at separate times. He had never been unfaithful to my knowledge, but he was really pushing me to get married. I was quite scared by the prospect because of my track record, and so far his hadn't been good, either.

After a few days of a very chilly atmosphere, he brought home a bottle of wine and flowers and what should have been a lovely proposal deteriorated into, "We either get married, or you piss off." Now, what girl could resist such romance? I drank the wine, put the flowers in a vase, and said I would think about it. We tentatively made plans to be married in April 1977, but I chickened out. I didn't really want to get married again because I couldn't see why we should. To be fair to Jim, I said I would think about it for a few months and then either make a commitment or move out. We agreed on August 1978 for our wedding.

By June my second marriage was looming, and I hoped that I wasn't making another mistake; I still didn't have the confidence in my own judgement to know one way or the other. I did feel differently about Jim, in that we had been through some rough times but he always backed me up in whatever decision was made. Jim passionately wanted to be married, whereas David had been lukewarm about the idea. My mother was predictably horrified that I was actually going to marry Jim, but it also suited her to know that I would no longer be living in sin.

Karen cried when I told her Jim and I were going to get married. It took me hours to get out of her what was making her so unhappy. She asked me why I had to have a different name than her, and she asked whether I would still be her mummy. It broke my heart that she was eight years old and had so much worry in her world. It took a lot of explaining to calm her down and reassure her that I would always be her mummy and that Daddy would always be her daddy, but Jim would be my husband. I didn't go into the step-brother thing—that would have been too much for her to cope with at the time.

For some months I had been working three nights a week at a local RSL club to get some extra money to pay for our wedding. Parents don't foot the bill for a second try. We had two of everything: two children, two mortgages, two cars, and two jobs each. Every spare bit of money earned went into the house, either in improvements or to pay off the mortgage.

We made sure we took Karen and Matthew on holiday once a year, and in 1978 we had already booked our holiday at a dude ranch in western NSW. We decided that we would make that our honeymoon and take both children with us. We had lived together for three years, so it wasn't as though we needed to get to know each other.

We decided to be married at home by a celebrant, and then we'd have our reception at the local club to which we both belonged. Our dining and lounge rooms were quite small, so we could only invite family and close friends to share our celebration. My aunty offered to ice the cake for our wedding as a gift, and Mum would supply the actual fruitcake. My mother was an excellent fruitcake cook, and the only two failures she had had were both my first and second wedding cakes. Make of that what you will.

I had a problem with what to wear because I was conscious of the fact that this was a second try for marital bliss. I brought home a full-skirted cream dress that I thought would be appropriate, but Jim took one look at it and said that he wanted me to be married in a long dress. Fortunately I could sew, and it was a frantic search for a suitable pattern that was not too bridal. A girl I worked with loaned me a pattern, Jim approved the design, and I came home from working at the RSL and started to cut it out on the floor. Two hours later it was all ready to be sewn up, and by the end of the weekend I had my dress completed and approved by the prospective bridegroom. At least this time I wouldn't have a dressmaking critic sitting in the front row.

I didn't trust my mother to just go with the flow. I knew she would have to throw a spanner in the works and mess up the plans somehow. Mum wanted to make Karen's dress, but I made sure it was in my hands well before the wedding day. I knew what she was capable of, with unpicking things at the last minute.

I had made arrangements for her to collect Karen at school at lunchtime on Friday and take her to the hairdressers. Unbeknownst to Mum, I had also made plan B, a later appointment at another hairdresser, because I didn't trust her to actually stick to plan A.

On the morning of the wedding, just before she was due to pick Karen up from school, I received a phone call from Dad telling me that Mum wouldn't be making the savouries she had promised, and she couldn't get to the school because she was too sick. No surprise there. Plan B came to the foreground again, and I got Jim to get Karen and take her to the hairdressers.

I had another phone call from Dad later in the afternoon to tell me that Mum was too sick to come to the wedding, and he would have to stay with her. I told him in no uncertain terms if he didn't come to the wedding, I would be really disappointed in him. He did turn up looking very sheepish, and later on he had to go home and collect Mum, who had apparently had a miraculous recovery, for the reception.

Proceedings got under way with Jim and I standing beside each other, Karen standing next to me, and Matthew standing next to Jim. It was Karen's job to hold my flowers, and Matthew held the cushion with our rings on it. The rings were tied on with satin ribbons, and once the rings had been removed, Matthew took great delight in swinging the cushion around by the ribbons. He got a sharp nudge in the shoulder from Jim, but with Matthew being Matthew, he was undeterred and continued on his merry way. Karen got the giggles that Matthew was getting into trouble, and the whole ceremony could have descended into chaos if it had been many minutes longer.

Mum sat at the main table with us, didn't eat her dinner, and wrapped up the chicken for the dog. She also had Karen sit on her lap for the two hours she was there, and then she took her back to her place, as previously arranged. Jim and I were going to have a weekend in the city and then take the kids on holiday for a week. This was my second wedding with no photos of the bridal party and parents, and I am certainly not going to go for the trifecta. I am done with weddings!

Kids on Honeymoon

We set off for our honeymoon at Mudgee the next morning with our two kids. At the dude ranch, Julie was keen to ride the horses, and Matthew didn't care where we were going. He liked animals, so I thought he would enjoy himself once we got there and he saw the dogs, cats, chickens, and sheep. I had been to this particular farm when Karen was about four years old, so I knew what the accommodations and layout of the farm was like.

There was a long drive up to the farmhouse with horse paddocks on one side and a pool and tennis court on the other. The farmhouse had a six-room motel attached for the guests. Each room had two bedrooms, a bathroom, and a small, convertible couch that could be used as a lounge or as an extra bed if needed. From the motel rooms, it was only a short step to the veranda, which ran around three sides of the farmhouse. The central portion was used for meals; it had a bar at the far end, and cowhide floor rugs and comfortable chairs abounded in front of the open fire. The veranda at the front of the house had a ping-pong table and a games area for the kids. The kids had to eat dinner early, and then it was happy hour for the adults with a children-free dinner. The children could either play in the veranda area or go back to their room in the motel section, but they were definitely not allowed in the dining room while their parents were having dinner.

At dinner on the first evening, we introduced ourselves, and the other guests asked how long we had been married. When we told them only three days, they were amazed that we would bring our children on our honeymoon. We had lived together since 1975, and it didn't seem like a honeymoon to us; rather, it was just another holiday with our children. I couldn't have left Karen with Mum for another week, or Karen would have been completely poisoned by the time we returned. Positive PR is not one of my mother's strong points.

There were plenty of activities each day for both adults and children. There were round-ups of sheep or cattle, all of which knew their way home. That was fortunate, because the way we went about rounding them up would have scattered them all over Mudgee! A hay ride was organised for the kids and those adults who didn't want to ride horses, or there were trail rides for the more adventurous. An egg collection competition each morning saw all these children running in amongst the hens with cries of "I've got one!" or, more often, "I've dropped one!" The kids thought it was great fun, but I don't think the hens enjoyed it much.

The families staying at the farm got along well, and there were a few children for each age group, so no child was left out. One of the chores performed on the farm was the slaughtering of the sheep and pigs, which was carried out by the owner of the property. Matthew wanted to go down to the slaughterhouse, but I felt he shouldn't. Somewhere he had managed to get hold of a packet of Smiths chips, and it was quite a picture seeing him standing there stuffing his face with chips while Vaughan slaughtered a sheep. I could only watch Matthew, not the slaughter, but he was completely undeterred. Nothing that happened on the farm seemed to worry him at all. Karen was another matter, and any form of what she perceived to be cruelty really upset her.

When horses were being allocated, Matthew was given Big Red, an ex-racehorse. He must have been all raced out, because he moved at a snail's pace. Matthew was told to steer him like he would steer a billy-cart, so Matthew took that instruction to the last letter. He held the reins as far apart as his five-year-old arms would go, and his legs stuck out at almost ninety degrees from the rather ample back of this huge horse. From his lofty perch of sixteen hands, Matthew would shout directions to the horse: "Move, Big Red!" or "Slow down, Big Red!" It took a bit of educating to teach him how to pull the reins to make the horse turn left or right. Big Red was a patient old horse and would happily amble along the bush tracks with Matthew on his back. His only problem was that another horse called Tipsy, who broke wind constantly, liked to walk behind Big Red and bite him on the rump. It was a highly amusing activity to get these trail rides under way. The horses had to go in the right order, or there would be chaos.

I was given Dolly, a thirty-five-year-old mare with a very strong will whose greatest delight of the day was trying to decapitate me as she raced across the home paddock and straight under the low roof of the shelter. Nothing would pull her up until she was under that sheet of tin. I also rode Coco, a chocolate and white pinto, who very unceremoniously dumped me in the middle of a ploughed field. The only thing hurt was my pride, but I got back on and continued the ride home.

Jim had a gelding named Noble, and noble the horse was not. He was a cranky, headstrong, and thoroughly disagreeable horse. Somehow Jim managed to keep him under control, but Noble got his own back. One of the stirrups snapped when they were about a half mile from home. Noble knew his jockey didn't have the same amount of control, so he broke into a gallop, and it was all Jim could do not to be thrown off as he clung precariously to the side of the horse.

Vaughan also taught me to ride bareback. Even though I am a Sagittarian and my star sign is half horse, I did not have a natural affinity with the equine. I was a little nervous of them, and they knew it, so the thought of riding one without the benefit of a saddle and reins was a little daunting. However, as I was always one to try anything once I decided to give it a go. It took a lot of concentration to follow Vaughan's instructions, but it was an exhilarating experience, and I thoroughly enjoyed it once the fear subsided.

Each evening at happy hour, we sat in the huge lounge room on the cowhide chairs and sipped on whatever concoction we cared to make up. Drinks were recorded on the honour system, and what you had was written down on a pad beside the bar, to be settled at the end of the holiday. Wine was served with dinner, and Mudgee has some superb vineyards, so a few of us decided to go out the next day and bring back a few cases of wine. Several of us set off after breakfast and visited a few of the local wineries, loading our purchases into the cars with the idea that we would take them home at the end of the holiday. That night we decided to let the other guests share in a sample of what we had bought. By the next morning we had none left, but we did have a monumental headache to show where the wine had gone!

After one of these extended happy hour dinners, we went to bed and could hear a lot of sheep quite close by, which was unusual. The next morning, as we came out of our room to go to breakfast, the whole tennis court was full of sheep. Vaughan had a cattle dog named Red who had helped his master out by bringing the sheep in and penning them in the tennis court. How that dog managed to get them in there remains a mystery. It took hours to sweep the sheep poo off the clay court, not to mention the effort involved in getting the sheep out of the court through one small gate.

It was a very happy week at Mudgee, but the time came to return to the Big Smoke and face the wrath of Doreen.

Dreams of a Water View, 1980-1985

 It had always been my father's dream to live near the water. My mother did not share that dream. Dad had worked hard all his life to provide a home and a good standard of living for his family, and he had decided to retire at sixty on the "burnt-out Digger's pension," as he affectionately called the Veterans Affairs fortnightly handout. He really wanted to build a house near the water, any water, but when he broached the subject to Mum, she flatly refused to consider the idea. Mum didn't like the water. She didn't want to be near, on, or in it, and she was terrified of being in a boat.

My father was still a very fit man and could outwork most men half his age, including my brother. Dad was not a devious person, but he wanted to fulfil his dream, so he started to put little bits of money aside in a secret bank account from part-time work that he managed to find. The land that he wanted was only seven thousand dollars because it was in an isolated spot and was only accessible by water. Barrier Point is on the Hawkesbury River, and the block he had chosen was about 250 feet from the shore. The land was so steep that the magnificent view was uninterrupted whichever way one looked. There was a cave right at the top of the block that seemed to have the remains of old cook fires deep within it. Local legend was that aborigines had inhabited the land and this was one of their shelters.

The land was cleared after many backbreaking hours of labour, and the house began. The holes were dug for the footings to take the pole uprights to support the frame and veranda of the house. It was then a matter of assembling the materials in Sydney needed for this huge project and getting them on site to Barrier Point, a journey by boat that was not to be undertaken by the faint hearted.

The design Dad chose for Barrier Point was an open-plan living area of lounge, dining room, and kitchen occupying one-half of the house; the other half contained two bedrooms and a bathroom. Across the back of the house was to be a wide deck that went as far as the steep rock wall would allow. The front would also have a deck about twelve feet wide to accommodate tables and chairs for outdoor dining, with wide eaves to keep the sun off the front windows. The house was level with the ground at the back, but it was some fifteen feet off the ground at the front; this gave enough room to accommodate a huge water tank and some storage space for tools. Dad had also decided to install an extra toilet and shower downstairs at a later date, as money permitted.

The house style lent itself to floor-to-ceiling glass windows and wide glass doors. The idea was that one could stand anywhere in the house and see the river. It was not necessary to have blinds or curtains because the house was so high that one would need to be in a helicopter to see into it. The wide eaves protected the front windows from the sun, and the slope of the land at the back protected the rear windows. The ceiling was pitched with roughly sawn beams inside, and suspended from the beams were ceiling fans. Two skylights were planned above the kitchen, and one went in the bathroom. Ferns in baskets were to be suspended below these skylights to take advantage of the natural light. The front bedroom faced the river, and Dad wanted the bed up on a platform so that he could lie in bed and see the water.

Furniture was to be comfortable and casual, with the minimum of housework involved. The kitchen was a U shape with the preparation bench facing the front of the house and the sink under the windows facing the back deck and garden. When he showed me the plans, I could visualise it in my mind and see what effect he wanted: sunny, airy, easy to clean, and comfortable.

To transport anything to Barrier Point required the materials to be loaded where they were purchased onto the empty boat trailer and delivered to Beresford. Then they had to be taken to Brooklyn and unloaded onto the wharf, which was a very rickety creation of all sorts of timber gathered over many decades. Between the pylons down each side, there were thick, chunky pieces running along the side of the wharf in an attempt to stop anyone falling off the edge. The planks running at right angles between these huge chunks were of varying width, thickness, and stability. Some had holes where the natural knot of the timber had long since fallen out, some had the remains of a previously used bolt still embedded in them, and others were warped and twisted. The sides had old tyres hanging along them on very thick slime-encrusted rope to stop the boats from being damaged if they should hit the wharf.

The ladder that disappeared over the side and into the dark green water made for precarious ascents and descents, but even more so when carrying timber over one's shoulder or when both hands were loaded with bags. As if this was not hazardous enough, it was necessary to dodge all the paraphernalia of a boat yard, with bits and pieces of working and non-working boat parts strewn on every bit of flat ground.

Added to this was the usual motley variety of cats that would run from everywhere to see what people had brought them to eat. They were the street urchins of the waterfront. They had natural survival instincts and knew when the possibility of a meal existed. Feed them once, and you were sunk! I am sure that one of them was delegated to take down car numbers so that when someone pulled into the car park, the call went out: "Dinner's on!"

Dad had a sixteen-foot, open aluminium boat with a Volvo motor and a centre steering console. This boat was moored some hundred feet off the shore at Brooklyn; this necessitated the use of a rowboat to get out to the mooring, and then we had to tow the rowboat back to the wharf, a procedure that usually took about half an hour in good conditions. Dad's boat was brought to the wharf, and we loaded the materials onto it. The trip from Brooklyn to Barrier Point took about thirty minutes, depending on the size and weight of the load.

The wharf at Barrier Point was another engineering masterpiece of the waterfront. It consisted of blocks of stone built out from the shoreline just high enough to be still visible in a king tide. The top of it was held together with a very doubtful mix of cement that had broken away along the edges, and the steps had long since lost their original level. They now leaned drunkenly to one side or the other, and the constant wash of the waves over the bottom few made exit from the boat a very tricky manoeuvre. Added to this architectural masterpiece were the green weeds that clung to the sides and tops of the bottom steps, ready to let the careless walker slide right back into the river. One had to time the natural wash of the waves, taking into account any wash from a passing boat. I'd poise myself on the nose of the boat (having nothing to hang onto) and make a graceful leap onto the steps without landing in the water. It was surprising how practice made perfect.

Once the human occupants were safely ashore, we unloaded the building materials and then carried them up a very steep hill to the building site. It was a very arduous task, but one that Dad attacked with enthusiasm. Quite a few friends and some residents of Barrier Point helped out with all this transporting of materials, and most of them never seemed to mind the work involved. In a settlement such as this, there was somebody building something at almost any given time, so it was a neighbourly thing to help each other. It also gave everyone a chance to swap tips about building on impossible sites, and there was never a shortage of opinions on how things should be done. There was usually a cup of tea, or something stronger if preferred, waiting at the end of the job. Sometimes there would be the chance for a break to go out and do a few hours of fishing—an activity almost worth the hard work preceding it.

Dad had always been a bit of a Steptoe, collecting all manner of bits and pieces. His garage looked like a second-hand building materials yard with the most unlikely combinations of timber, pipe, metal, and paint. Somehow he always found a use for most things, and he was particularly fond of oversize pieces of timber. If a job called for 3" × 2", it was not unusual for Dad to use a 6" × 4", just to be sure. We used to call him Oversize Alf, but anything he built never fell down. It didn't matter to him if the timber had drill holes or metal still screwed to it—he would find a use for it so that nothing went to waste.

Dad had heard that one could get second-hand traffic light poles from the Roads and Traffic Authority, and he decided to use these as the supports for the floor of the house. They were ideal for the job because they were cheap, and wouldn't rot. The fact that they were cheap was the primary factor, I suspect. The footings were dug, the concrete was poured, and the poles were set. Next came the bearers and joists for the floor. The Council was not happy about the use of second-hand building materials in case there were flaws in them. I think Dad managed to sneak a few in here and there where he didn't think they would be seen. The frame of the house was pre-fab metal, and it was brought in by helicopter and lowered on site.

The neighbours were a friendly bunch of people for the most part, and Dad had a great guy living next door. Don Read had lived at Barrier Point for a few years, and his house style was similar to Dad's but with a much smaller front veranda. Don and Dad shared many happy hours talking about old times. When the house was in its early stages, only a platform and frame, Don and his friend Laura gave Dad a bed for the night so that he could get in a few days' work at a time. They would often call him in for a cuppa or a cold beer while he was working, and their hospitality and friendship certainly made the job easier for him.

Mum refused to have anything to do with this dream home of Dad's, and she did everything in her power to make life difficult for him. One of things she did was take as much money out of their shared bank account as possible, so that he would not be able to draw on it for the house. Messages for Dad from various contractors were left with Mum in his temporary absence, but she never passed them on to him. There was a very bad storm up at Brooklyn, and Dad's boat broke away from its mooring. The owner of the boatshed rang Mum and told her what had happened. This message was not passed on, and when Dad drove up with a load of building materials, he found out his boat had been tied up somewhere downriver. He was furious and abused the boatshed owner for not letting him know the boat was missing, but when he found out the truth, of course he didn't express any of this anger to Mum when he got home.

It was a battle of wills between Mum and Dad to get this house built. Dad was trying to do a bit of part-time work to earn some money for the house, and Mum's campaign included not cooking his meals or doing his washing. This meant that if Dad wanted to go up to Barrier Point for a few days to do more building, then he had to take care of his own domestic routines at home. I felt sorry for Dad because he was being punished for fulfilling his dream, when all his life he had worked for his family and had denied us nothing. I thought it was about time he got something that he wanted, and I supported what he was doing. This attitude of mine naturally did not please my mother. I had to do what I felt was right, so Jim and I started to go up to Barrier Point on weekends and give Dad some help with the house. The trips caused endless tirades of abuse by my mother, but by the age of thirty-five I was becoming somewhat immune to them. I cooked meals for Dad that could be shared with Don and Laura, because his house was not to the stage that there was power connected or any cooking facilities. The only electricity source for the house was an extension lead run from Don's place so that Dad could use his power tools. When Dad came back to Sydney after working on the house, I helped out with his washing, often putting him up for the night and cooking some casseroles that he could share with the neighbours.

There were many trips up the Hawkesbury, the boat loaded to the gunwhales with building materials. Dad, Karen (who was about eleven), and I made one particularly memorable trip surrounded by aluminium windows and doors, with no room left to sit on the seats. Stacked across the front of the boat were sheets of corrugated iron, and when another boat passed us, the wash came right up the sides and into the boat. The trip was slow and very scary, and there were moments when I was sure we would sink. We couldn't even get to the lifejackets if they were needed; they were tucked securely under the nose of the boat. I was so glad to get back on dry land.

When we reached Hawko's Wharf at Barrier Point, the contents of the boat had to be unloaded and stacked on the wharf so that they were ready to be carried up the hill. The public wharf was a much more substantial structure than Hawko's Wharf with a fairly decent-sized wooden platform onto which one could step from the boat with a reasonable amount of safety. It even had handrails up the side of the steps. The windows and doors were heavy, but between the three of us we managed to carry them all up the hill. Karen overbalanced and put her foot right through one of the windows, but fortunately she wasn't cut by the broken glass.

It was about this time that some of the residents decided they needed an easier way of transporting goods from the wharf to the homes of the growing community. Added to this was the fact that none of them were getting any younger, and at times the household shopping meant many trips back and forth to the wharf. I suspect it was probably those residents who also included many cases of beer in their essential food shopping who were at the forefront of the push to obtain a vehicle. An old Holden of the mid-1950s vintage was obtained from goodness knows where and brought up to Barrier Point by barge. It did not need to be registered because somebody had the bright idea that it would be good for carting water to fight any bushfires that may break out. Registration problem solved! The roof of the car was unceremoniously removed with an angle grinder, and it became something of a convertible. It was not quite car, not quite utility, not quite truck, but useful. It was wonderful to be able to back it down to the edge of the wharf and load on cans of paint, tiles, and even some small pieces of furniture. It was then only a matter of then carting the load up into the house.

Every single thing had to be transported by this cumbersome method of several loadings and unloadings. Even the huge water tank had to be floated upriver. I spent one weekend painting it with a two-inch brush, and almost as soon as I finished, Dad found a four-inch brush that would have made a much quicker job.

It seemed to take months to get enough material up there to finish the next part of the job. By the time three years had passed, the house was to the lock-up stage and was starting to resemble something in which one could actually live. The hours spent up there never felt like a chore; it was more like realising a long-held dream.

We used to take some mince outside in the late afternoon and feed the kookaburras. They were always pleased to see any kind of human habitation because it meant an easy dinner for them. They became quite tame and sometimes could be hand fed, but not if they had young ones about. There were also parrots and the inevitable magpies that would try to freeload. Black cockatoos took up residence in the casuarina trees at the back of the block, and they would make such a racket in the late afternoon and early morning. In addition to feathered wildlife, there was often a snake or lizard around the water tank, particularly in the dry weather. It paid to watch where one put one's feet.

While Dad was still building up at Barrier Point, I was working for a surgeon at Bankstown. He had bought a house that needed some renovations to convert it into a medical practice. Simple things such as moving doorways, installing air conditioners, and fitting the office with some cupboards and shelving could be done by a carpenter. The bigger jobs such as concrete driveways and carports, electrical changes, and plumbing would need an expert. Dad needed some money to finish his house, so I suggested to Chris, the surgeon, that he let Dad handle the renovations. I knew he wasn't brilliant as a carpenter, but the work required would be within his capabilities. It was my job to coordinate the project and have it finished for opening the first week of January; all that Chris did was sign the cheques. He left everything else up to me, including getting plans drawn up and obtaining Council permission to convert a somewhat plain weatherboard house into a functional doctor's surgery.

My brother was coerced into helping, but that was a disaster! Dad had never heard of straight or level and simply cut holes or hammered nails where he thought it would be okay. Charlie was very offended by this lack of precision, and he and Dad had many a fallout over their different styles of carpentry. After all, my brother had done his apprenticeship with a reproduction furniture company and worked to the nearest millimetre, whereas Dad worked to the nearest centimetre. My brother had had enough one day when he tried to hang doors on an opening that leaned drunkenly to one side. He threw his hammer down and left, never to return to the building site.

It was quite a challenge, but it was one that I relished. It was finished on time, and the weekend before we were due to open for business in the new premises, a large number of people carted boxes of files and records from one surgery suite to the other. There was probably only 250 yards between the two locations, but it necessitated transporting everything down two flights of stairs, out of the old building, up the street, and into the new premises.

The Sunday of that weekend, Dad and I put the plants in the rockery out in the front of the new surgery, in the pouring rain. We were dressed in old clothes and had our heads and shoulders covered with black garbage bags. We were both exhausted by the end of the day, but we were extremely pleased with ourselves that we had managed to get it all done. Chris had also agreed for Dad to stay on and maintain the lawns and gardens as required, clean the surgery, and wash his Mercedes each week. The extra money that Dad had earned meant that he could finish off his house, even if Mum made it difficult with the finances.

My mother still didn't want to have anything to do with the house, and the relationship between her and I was strained, to say the least. She felt that I was taking Dad's side—and I was. I felt that he was entitled to do what he was doing, and he wasn't causing any harm to anyone. It was great to get up there on weekends, even though we worked most of the time. There were days when we'd put down the tools and take the boat out fishing, usually bringing home enough for a feast.

I was nearly forty, and Dad and I were finally getting to know each other. We enjoyed each other's company. I also saw more of him now that he was working part-time at the surgery. When up at Barrier Point, we worked side by side doing very hard physical labour, and I revelled in the challenge of helping to turn a steep block of land into a home and outdoor area that was beautiful. We would discuss a certain part of the house or the garden and how it should look, and then we'd set about achieving that aim. I never minded how early we started each day, how long we worked, or how hard. It was the sense of accomplishment that made it all worthwhile.

Hawko's Wharf had seen better days, and it was about this time that Jim got the opportunity to buy a disused pontoon from the navy. It was ideal for mooring the boat and could also be used by some of the other residents to moor theirs. It was towed by barge up to Barrier Point and then ceremoniously anchored firmly to the bottom of the river. Permission was obtained from the Maritime Services, Lands Department, and Council so that a new wooden wharf could be constructed from the shore out into the river. This new wharf and the attached pontoon would provide mooring for several boats, and the residents interested in the project paid their share of the cost. It was such an improvement on the rickety structures that were in abundance along the waterfront, and it was quite a grand sight. It even had lights so that one could walk along it safely at night, although the condition of some of the residents after a night at Moonee Moonee Workers Club would defy safety by any sort of lighting.

Dad had always been a good fisherman, and he tried to teach Jim how to fish, but somehow they always seemed to disagree on the best tackle to use. Oversize Alf carried the idea of "bigger is better" through to his fishing rig, and he seemed to be of the opinion that if the hook was large, he would only catch big fish. This generally proved to be true. The sinkers were enormous, and the lines seemed to be like thin rope. Once something was hooked, it would be caught with no chance of breaking the fishing lines. We barbecued many a bream only hours after they came out of the water, still shiny and smelling of the salt; the memory of these fresh fish remains today. It rather spoiled one's appetite for fish bought from a shop.

As the house slowly but surely became more liveable, Dad talked Mum into going up there one weekend. It was a case of, "If you can't beat them, join them." From then on, everything changed. It was as a though a cloud had descended over the house, and all the joy and happiness evaporated. The happy, relaxed atmosphere disappeared like the morning mist, and in its place was a feeling of disapproval and impatience that it had not been done "her way". Even the concept of the house was altered because Mum didn't like there being no blinds on the windows and no covers on the skylights. The idea of putting a bed on a platform was ridiculous to her way of thinking. The front room had a double bed, and the second room two single beds, one designated for Karen and the other for Mum.

The living area was designed to have the lounge face the windows so that one could see the view. Mum didn't think that was a good idea, so the lounge furniture was moved over into the corner. She didn't like the idea of the neighbours being able to see in the side window (the neighbours were about fifty feet away), so she bought a roll-down blind—second-hand, of course. Curtains went up at the kitchen window, blinds were bought for the front, and covers were made for the skylights. The house that had been designed to be airy and spacious was being turned into a fortress, and its intended character was being lost. Dad had sacrificed the peace and serenity of the house at Barrier Point, hoping that Mum would like it there and give him peace at home. He never learned that giving in to my mother never brought peace.

There was a gap of about ten feet between the back door and the rocks and dirt that formed the hill behind the house. After much deliberation between Dad, Jim, and me, we decided to put a deck right across the back of the house, some thirty-three feet by ten feet, and a terrace and a rockery up the hill. At the end of the deck and outside the kitchen, Dad wanted to have a covered area with glass walls that enclosed part of the rockery; he wanted to be able to see past the rockery up the hill. A corrugated iron roof that sloped away from the house and out over the deck achieved this purpose. Glass doors from an old chemist shop were positioned at an angle of about forty-five degrees, but they did not touch the ground, allowing the rockery to be built from the edge of the deck up to the doors and continue beneath the doors into the bush beyond. It gave a spectacular result and looked beautiful when planted with azaleas, ferns, and other rockery plants, giving a mix of colours and leaf textures.

The sheltered area near the back door was an ideal place for a beer fridge, and Dad obtained one, though I didn't know from where. Mum of course did not want this to be just a beer fridge—that was an absolute waste of good space, as far as she was concerned. She was not happy until she had the freezer full of extra tubs of margarine and frozen peas, so that eventually there was no room to store any surplus fish that Dad might catch. She didn't like fish, anyway.

The back deck was also fitted out with yellow light globes as mosquito repellents, and it was lovely to sit outside at dusk and have a cold drink while we waited for the steak or fish to cook on the barbecue. My mother was not a member of the great outdoors way of thinking, and she would try to get us to eat dinner inside; sometimes she won. Most times we preferred to eat outside because it was so pleasant on the deck. The next-door neighbour played all types of music, but we particularly enjoyed some of the old-time dance records. We would clap loudly when he played something we liked, and he would put his head out the door and shout, "Do you want to hear that again?" Hawko and his wife had a great collection of records, and we were lucky enough to be able to share their music. At that stage we did not have a sound system, just a portable radio that was not quite in the same league as Hawko's stereo.

Stairs were also needed from the deck up into the bush, and Dad achieved this by taking stone from the hill and packing down dirt to make steps. Dad and I worked all one weekend on this project, and we were totally in agreement on how it should look: totally natural. Next to these stairs a barbecue was made, set into the hill and positioned about waist high. Jim had the plate made for Dad, and many a fish was fried only hours after being caught. Jim had developed a stuffing for the fish that consisted of breadcrumbs, lemon juice, lemon rind, capsicum, minced onion, and a bit of butter. All of this was stuffed into the cavity of the fish before it was wrapped in oiled aluminium foil and barbecued.

The remainder of the hill, which ran along behind the bedrooms, was terraced and planted with native plants. Some were ground covers, some were low growers, and some were small trees. They were chosen to complement each other, and they looked as though they had always lived there. Dad spent hundreds of dollars on plants, and again they had to be transported by boat and carried up the hill; the boat looked like a floating jungle on that particular trip. My mother again had an opinion about how the garden should look, and she proceeded to plant parsley and ribbon grass amongst all the native plants. Needless to say, within a short time these horticultural nightmares had almost taken over, and the natural look of the garden was spoilt.

The kitchen, which had been pulled out of a house, was given to Dad for a very good price—free. It had timber-tone, laminated doors and was in particularly good condition. It was unbelievable that it fit almost perfectly in the area designated and hardly had to be altered. Even the colours were complementary to the rest of the decor. Dad and I spent a week in the house installing the kitchen and laying the floor tiles. This necessitated nailing two-foot square pieces of masonite over the floorboards to give a flat surface and then crawling around on hands and knees to stick the floor tiles down. My knees were so sore by the end of that particular job that I was extremely glad the bedrooms were going to have carpet.

About this time, Mum had a firm hold on what the house should look like, and it differed greatly from the original concept. Dad, as per usual, did anything for the sake of peace. He read the *Trading Post* paper each week looking for second-hand furniture bargains, and we succeeded in getting some really nice wardrobes from a family at West Ryde. Mum didn't like the colour, of course. When the bedroom furniture was to be bought, even though she was not sleeping in that room, Mum did not want the double bed on a platform, so it wasn't. The single beds in the second bedroom were primarily outfitted with linen from home. A chest of drawers and small wardrobe were installed, and she filled them with clothes that she did not usually wear. She had designated which drawers were hers and which were Karen's. Jim and I didn't figure in the distribution of wardrobe space, and it was becoming more obvious that Mum didn't expect us to be holidaying there.

Matthew, Jim's son, stayed with us most weekends in Sydney, and Mum had taken a particular dislike to him. She therefore demanded that when Jim, Karen, Matthew, and I went to Barrier Point for the weekend, Matthew was not to sleep in *her* bed. The sleeping arrangements were to be Jim and I in the double bed, Karen in her designated bed, and Matthew sleeping in the lounge. I couldn't believe that she actually thought we would agree with this and continue to go up there to work. Not one weekend did we spend there holidaying.

There was a photo frame hanging on the wall in the hallway between the bathroom and the second bedroom. In that frame there were photos of my parents, my brother and his family, and me, Jim, Karen, and Matthew. It was not long before Mum ripped the photos of Jim and Matthew from the frame. It was such a stupid and childish thing to do, but it was very hurtful to me.

My mother always took more food up for the weekend than the occupants could possibly eat. Everything had to be transported from the boat to the house, and from the house to the boat for the return trip, so it was really annoying to have cart this food up the hill knowing that in thirty-six hours we would be taking most of it back!

Clothing was another hassle. Mum would not simply pack a bag for the amount of time she would be at Barrier Point. There were clothes in the wardrobe, but because they were things she had not worn at home, there was very little likelihood of her wearing them at Barrier Point. This meant that bags of clothes went up, and bags of clothes came home. She would not wash them out and leave them there; the same applied to the bed linen and towels. We carted clean laundry up the hill, and we carted dirty washing back down the hill. It was absolutely ridiculous, and I expressed my opinion on that subject several times. I felt I had a right to because I was doing a large share of the carting.

Jim and I could no longer go to Barrier Point by simply making arrangements with Dad. Mum was in charge of the visiting roster, and we were not welcome. I had gone against her wishes too many times, and it was time for her to get even. On one occasion, we had made arrangements to go to Barrier Point with some friends, and at the last minute we were advised rather sheepishly by Dad that Mum wanted to go up there, so we couldn't. I was really upset about this because we had spent nearly five years working hard on weekends and holidays, and just when the house was becoming habitable, we were being edged out.

Even though my relationship with my father had blossomed and strengthened over the years we had been building Barrier Point, my mother's emotional hold on him was stronger. She was the more powerful personality and had battle tactics that I had never even dreamed of.

Dad very reluctantly let us go to Barrier Point on the weekends that he was *absolutely sure* that Mum would not want to go there. He was caught in the crossfire again, but it was of his own making. I still allowed Karen to see her grandparents, and she went to their house straight after school one day a week. She stayed for tea, went to physical culture with Mum, and stayed overnight. Dad was still working on the house at Barrier Point, and he also did some part-time work in Sydney. Unfortunately the night Karen stayed at their house was usually Monday, and that happened to be one of the days that Dad was at Barrier Point because he would stay for a few days after the weekend. It was not my fault that it fell that way, but Dad blamed me for the fact that he was not seeing Karen.

One night I had let Karen go to Mum and Dad's for tea because it was Karen's fourteenth birthday that week. On the way home in the car, Karen said to me that she didn't know how I could be so horrible to her grandparents and treat them like I did. I was upset and angry, and as I was driving, I let go with my left hand and hit her across the face. I didn't know who got the biggest shock. She was horrified that I had hit her, and I was just as horrified that I had exhibited behaviour that I found abhorrent in my mother. I apologised profusely, but nothing was going to change the fact that I had unfairly hit my daughter.

In late April 1984, Jim was away on an army camp, and we had arranged to go to Barrier Point for a week when he came back. The house was finally habitable, and I was looking forward to being out on the river or going for a walk along the waterfront. Being away from the traffic of Sydney and relaxing would be heaven.

There was a knock on my front door, and when I opened it, my father stood on the doorstep. "I've come to get the keys of Barrier Point from you," he said.

I couldn't believe my ears. This time we were effectively being stopped from even getting into the house. I was so shocked that I stammered, "I don't know where they are. I'll have to look for them and give them to you later." He stood there looking very uncomfortable. He constantly moved from foot to foot as if he would rather be anywhere than standing on my doorstep. "Why are you doing this to me?" I said.

He replied, "You are stopping me from seeing Karen, so I am stopping you from going to Barrier Point." No amount of explaining on my part was going to change things, so I simply shut the door and went inside. I then threw myself on the bed and cried.

After a little while, I decided that crying wasn't going to achieve anything, so later that night I looked for the keys. I drove over to my parents' house and stood outside the gate at the steps to their front veranda. Nobody was home, so I hurled the keys as far up the veranda as they would go and turned around and left. I cried all the way home and could hardly see the road through my tears.

Jim was away, and I spent a very sleepless and teary night trying to come to terms with my anger, frustration, and disappointment. I couldn't believe that my father had been so weak as to succumb to my mother's pressure and effectively stop us from using the house we loved so much. Throughout that night I resolved that I would not go without a holiday, even though it could no longer be at Barrier Point.

The next day I went to the NRMA and booked a week at Lakeside Caravan Park. I wanted to be within two hours of Sydney, because Jim was coming back from two weeks of driving trucks for the army, and he probably wouldn't want to do a long trip.

When he came home, I told him what had happened, and he was speechless and then very angry. "How could your old man be so weak?" he raged. "Your mother finally got her way. I hope the bitch is satisfied." He was disgusted with my father and contemptuous of my mother. He couldn't believe that we had been thrown out just when we could start to enjoy the fruits of our labour.

In November 1984 Mum and I were discussing the arrangements for Christmas Day over the phone. I asked her if she would like to come to my place for lunch, and her reply was, "I am not going to have lunch with that mongrel and his bastard son (Matthew). I'll leave your presents on the front fence."

I told her, "If you can't be bothered to come and at least have a cup of tea with me on Christmas Day, then you can shove your presents, and I don't want to talk to you ever again." I was so hurt. What right did she have to speak about Jim and Matthew like that? What I had done to deserve this kind of abuse was to help my father against her wishes. I didn't see her or speak to her on Christmas Day for the next five years. My mother had achieved her hidden agenda: take over Barrier Point, keep Jim and me away from the house, and break up my burgeoning relationship with my father.

Ten years later, during Easter 1994, we decided to have a day out on the Hawkesbury River with some friends. We took the opportunity to stop at Barrier Point and see what had happened in the previous decade.

My parents no longer owned the house. My father's dream home had been sold because my mother didn't want to travel there by boat, and because there were no shops. She had managed to convince him that a holiday house somewhere else would be preferable—for her. Like a fool, he went along with it. Would this man never learn?

The search had started in 1986 for a block of land, and Mum's criteria was "close to shops and able to drive to the front door". Unbeknownst to Mum, Dad found a steep block at Ulara, right near the top of a hill and accessed by a short private road. He bought it without her prior approval. I am convinced that my father had never in his life considered the possibility of building on a flat block of ground. This was the third one that required the climbing skills of a mountain goat, but this time he would not have his daughter and son-in-law to help; I was no longer speaking to them and only knew about the land from my brother. A kit home was chosen with certain modifications, and he commenced building.

Prior to completion of the house at Ulara, my father had a cerebral haemorrhage and never got the chance to use it.

We Won't Be Beaten

When Jim and I took our vacation at Lakeside Caravan Park, we loved the place from the first moment we drove through the gate. I had never spent much time in caravan parks because my parents tended to go for motel or house accommodation for our holidays, so this would be a fairly unique experience. I had requested an on-site van with its own en-suite, and the one we were allocated was on the edge of the reserve fronting onto the lake.

The van was nothing fancy, but it was clean and big enough for Jim and me. The breeze from the lake was beautiful, and we had the reserve in front of us that we could use for barbecues. We unpacked our clothes, made the bed, and went for a walk through Lakeside Leisure Park. The park was full of beautiful trees and gardens and abundant with bird life. Singles, couples, and families walked throughout the park and some children rode bicycles or tried to stay upright on skateboards.

There were two pools, one for adults and a wading pool for the kids. Beside the pools was a tennis half-court, and across the road was the office, shop, and movie theatre. The park was set out with roads running across the width and joined at each end by the main road, which almost encircled the park. The amenities block with showers, toilets, and laundry was in the middle. Up the back of the park and before the camping area, there was a BMX bike track and a children's play area. A large community hall was the last building and was used for bingo nights, country dances, and parties. There was so much to do at Lakeside, and we were really happy that we had booked there.

The second day we decided to go for a walk and see what types of other accommodations the park offered. Some of the caravans were well cared for with potted plants out the front and a chair or two for sitting in the sunshine. There was a mixture of vans with canvas annexes, large mobile homes with metal annexes, and caravans that were rarely used by the owners and were parked in a sad little huddle at the back of the park, brought to a site only when the owner's arrival was imminent.

As we walked around, we started to talk. "You know," I said, "I wouldn't mind having a place here."

"I was just thinking the same thing myself," Jim replied. It was then we decided to find out what was available to buy. We went back down to the office and spoke to the receptionist, Lyn. "Could we have a look at some places that are for sale?" we inquired. "What price range did you have in mind?" she asked.

"We don't know. We haven't any idea what they are worth," Jim informed her.

Lyn quoted a price range between seven and eighteen thousand dollars, and to us this seemed an affordable amount. She gave us the keys to several with the comment, "Once you have looked at number twenty-five, you won't be interested in any of the others."

She was absolutely right. Some of those vans for sale were so small I would have to ask the other person to go outside so that I could turn around. I couldn't stand living in conditions so cramped—I liked my space.

We stood outside number twenty-five and really liked what we saw. It was a cream van with a cream metal annex. A sliding glass door at the front opened out onto a small veranda with a set of three steps down to the ground. The annex had windows along the side, and the whole van looked to be in really good condition. We went up the steps, opened the door, and fell in love with what we hoped would be our new holiday home. The sliding glass doors at the front of the annex opened into the lounge room, which had a bedroom behind it. The van part of the setup had an archway from the lounge room into the kitchen and dining room. Also off the lounge room was a doorway that led into the bathroom, and another door led to the main bedroom. The walls inside the van were light-coloured imitation timber panelling, and all the windows were aluminium. The carpet was pale beige, and all the furniture was in tones of brown and matched nicely. It was clean, bright, and airy. The only two things I didn't like were the curtains (easily changed) and two pictures of red chooks on the back wall. They had to go!

There was a large refrigerator in the kitchen, an LPG stove, and plenty of cupboards. The bathroom was a very good size and had a moulded shower/bath, vanity unit, and toilet. Although there was no back door, there was a large area at the back, which we decided could be concreted to give us somewhere to put our barbeque, tables, and chairs. It was an ideal site with a large area at the side for parking the car and a paddock behind us so that we had a fair amount of privacy—for a caravan park.

The whole thing was perfect. The only problem was, where were we going to get the money to buy it? We returned the key to Lyn at the office. "Well, what did you think?" she asked.

"You were right. Once we had seen number twenty-five, no other place got a look," I replied. We obtained the owners' telephone number and rang them to see if they would reduce the price, but they were quite adamant that it was worth what they were asking. We agreed with them, but there was no harm in asking. The next problem was financing the sale. Jim rang the credit union, and after many more phone calls and long-distance negotiating, the finance was arranged. According to the powers that be at the credit union we were not really in a position to afford the van because we already had a loan with them. However, they did agree to add the balance owing onto the new loan and let us pay it all off together. The van was ours!

All this negotiating took place in the week that we spent at Lakeside, supposedly on holidays. Once we had seen the van, we didn't want to miss out on buying it, and we were especially looking forward to being able to spend time there with the kids. Over the previous years, we had become used to being away on weekends, and we really enjoyed it. Lakeside Leisure Park would be significantly different to Barrier Point because we could drive to the door, and there was no mountain to lug our groceries and clothes up when we arrived. That would be the only thing I would miss about Barrier Point.

When we got back to Sydney after our holiday, I went to K-mart and bought new bed linen, towels, sheets, dinner sets, cutlery, and a myriad other household bits and pieces. Some things I could spare from home, but I certainly didn't have enough bedding to supply two houses. I accumulated groceries and raided the cupboards at home to provide food for the new place. We loaded everything onto our box trailer, and away we went to Lakeside.

Matthew and Karen instantly liked the place and set off to explore. They were quite satisfied that there was plenty for them to do, and they had also sighted quite a few young people around their ages, thirteen and fifteen. This place definitely had possibilities for some good weekends and holidays, and we could invite our friends up to stay whenever it suited us. We no longer had to go through my mother as the booking clerk.

We met our neighbours, Ron and Judy, who lived in the park permanently. They were the kind of people one instantly liked. Ron, an ex-truckie, was a big man with a very craggy, lived-in face, and he was rather keen on a beer. Judy was about five feet five and had a cuddly stature, with warm brown eyes and dark curly hair. She had the cleanest van I had ever seen. Judy and a duster were very good mates! We felt lucky to have neighbours who were such nice people, and they assured us that they would keep an eye on the van while we were not there. It wasn't long before we gave Judy a key, and she would go in periodically and check that everything was all right.

The neighbours on the other side were "casuals" like us, and it was some weeks before we actually got to meet them. They were in the process of trying to sell their van and only came up every so often. There seemed to be a mix of permanents and casuals in the park, and over the next few weeks we made friends with several couples, as well as widowed women and men, who lived near our site. Most of the people lived there because they either couldn't afford a house or preferred the community feeling of a caravan park. There was a very friendly atmosphere about the place, and it was nice to be able to go for a walk and see people who actually spoke to you, who didn't put their heads down and hurry past.

The first item on the agenda was to convert the exterior plug-in power cables to a safer way of delivering electricity to the van. The inherited system was extension leads plugged into an outside power source, then draped across fresh air through the window of the van and into the interior power point. It was not a very satisfactory system because there had been occasions where other people had had the exterior plug pulled out of the power source while they were absent; this generally resulted in a fridge full of spoilt food, not to mention the smell! Jim ran our power through a conduit and up through the floor of the van. It was constructed so that the plug could not be pulled out of the exterior power source. This also meant that Ron and Judy could walk down the side of their van without worrying about getting beheaded by the cable strung to our van. It was a stupid arrangement that each van's power source was in a neighbour's yard—very bad planning on the park management's part.

We had a small slab of concrete in our "yard" at the side of the van, and this was to be the next project. It needed to be increased in length and also extended across to the steps so we could get from the car to the van without getting muddy feet. This side of the van was the low side of the land, and water tended to collect there and create a bit of a quagmire. Adding to this problem was the position of the water tap: it stood on a piece of pipe about three feet out of the ground and right in the middle of our piece of yard. It was often left dripping by people using it and caused a mud puddle underneath. It could not have been put in a more inconvenient place, and we wanted it relocated. The park manager was not really interested in organising the work, so Jim asked if we could do it ourselves. He reluctantly agreed, so we moved it over to the side, giving us a clear bit of space in the centre of the yard.

All of this work took many weeks and several of the residents came and inquired about what we were doing. They were most interested in why "casuals" would bother to go to all this trouble. The majority of people in the park had a "gypsy" mentality and felt that there was no point putting in plants, no point in doing anything permanent because you might get thrown out of the park next week. Everything they did around their van could be packed and moved at very short notice, such as pot plants, chairs, portable clothes lines, etc. Nobody else had extended their parking space, and several of them did not even have cement to park on—just two tyre tracks. Many of the vans had been there for years, yet the owners still maintained this "portability" mentality. We had no intention of moving anywhere for quite some time and wanted our van to be as comfortable as possible.

We had no back door and therefore had to come out through the front, down the steps, and around the side of the annex to reach our slab of cement. This was all right in the summer, but in the winter or after heavy rain, there was a muddy track down the side of the annex, which meant a veranda full of shoes, or mud on the carpet—neither of which was a good option. Project number three: make a path from the front steps around to the backyard. By this time the residents of the park thought we were slightly mad to keep spending money on a van that we didn't even live in permanently!

Once again we had to see the park manager and ask if we could build a path down the side of the annex. "If you draw up a plan of what you want and give it to me, I will ask the park owner," he said. We did as he asked. This was not just an ordinary path but was being built mainly to solve the problem of the ground water. I had designed a path that incorporated gravel about a foot deep, contained on one side by the cement slab underneath the annex and on the other side by Koppers logs. For stepping stones, we wanted to put circles of tree trunks so that we would not have to walk on the gravel in bare feet. The Koppers logs fence would start off short at the front and increase to about two feet high at the back of the block, where the path widened out to form a semicircular garden. I wanted to plant some native shrubs to bring the birds around.

This was a very radical idea in an area that had a portability mentality. Permanent trees and a permanent path were beyond most of the residents' comprehension. The owner agreed to us doing this work because she could see that it would be an improvement, and even if we did leave, it would be an asset to the next people coming into the park. Jim and I took a week's holiday and spent the time constructing this path and garden. The owner generously agreed to us using some road base that was dumped at the back of the camping area. It was what they used in any cementing in the park, and it was more than useful for what we wanted to do. We were grateful for the offer and made the most of it.

The next week we came back with a trailer load of plants, and the result was terrific. It was just what we had wanted to achieve, and it solved the problem of the muddy track from the door of the van to the backyard. While we were in working mode, we also decided to extend the back concrete slab behind the annex. We took the cement out far enough to be able to fit a gas barbecue, tables, and chairs on it, and we built up the garden around the melaleucas to finish it off. Behind the van there was already a small piece of concrete that was an extension of the slab beneath the van, and we used this to put our spare beer fridge. Our site backed onto a paddock, and we had no power on the outside of the van, so we decided to put a Portaflood light above the barbecue—more consternation by the residents. There was no work we did that didn't attract a gallery of opinions. They even inspected what we had done in our absence, and they had a myriad advice ready for us on our return. They meant well, but after a while it really started to get on our nerves.

Within twelve months of us creating the path, garden, and outdoor eating area, some of the residents decided that it was such a good idea they might do some improvements, too. We helped at least three permanents improve their outdoor area, and the park manager was more than happy for us to do it. After all, it was a definite upgrade from the usual horticultural attempts of fifty faded, tattered plastic pots filled with half-dead and very unsuitable plants stacked across the front of vans and hanging from the tow bars.

We had made many friends in the park during the time we had spent at Lakeside, and through one such couple we bought a boat. Daisy and Ron Cocker lived two streets up from us, and they were a couple of characters. Daisy was tall, blonde, and an English ex-barmaid; everyone was "luv" to her. She had a particular thirst for gin and orange, and almost any time of the day she could be found with a glass of this concoction not more than an arm's length away. She had a really good heart and would help anyone, anytime. Ron was ex-British Navy and was a one-man circus. I don't think he really meant to be funny, but he was. He wasn't very tall and was very slightly built, and he could hardly be seen over the dashboard of the big Valiant he drove.

Ron's brother-in-law David had a boat he wanted to sell, and we were in the market to buy one. Ron arranged for us to meet David, who took Jim out in the boat, off the beach at Terrigal. The boat performed beautifully and only had sixty hours on the engine's clock. We couldn't afford what he wanted for the boat, but after a bit of haggling he agreed to let us have it for our price. He was selling it with all the equipment and even gave us a set of water skis and ropes, because his children no longer used them. We were thrilled. Now Jim could go fishing, and Karen and Matthew could learn to ski. We named the boat WOFTAM, an army term for a "Waste of

F*#^ing Time and Money", but we never got around to having the sign written. Maybe that was just as well.

Owning the boat also meant that Jim was the only one with a current licence, which he had obtained while we were going to Barrier Point. He had needed it then to drive Dad's boat, either with a load on or for fishing. Karen, Matthew, and I enrolled for a course at the Volunteer Coast Guard to get our boat licences, which we subsequently achieved. I was not all that keen on driving the boat and was always a bit nervous about handling the controls, especially at speed. I hated the thought of hitting something and sinking because I hadn't remembered the rules. I also mistrusted the ability of other boatees because we had had a few narrowly avoided mishaps with ski boats not doing the right thing. They seemed to think that because they had huge, inboard motors, they owned the lake and could do what they liked.

We bought Matthew and Karen wetsuits so that they could learn to ski. They had met up with a young fellow named Andrew, whose parents had a huge ski boat with a very powerful motor, and he seemed to be fairly skilled at skiing. He had a single ski that was very slimline and sprayed silver, and he had christened it Baby. He offered to teach the kids to ski and spent many hours patiently helping them. Matthew took to it fairly fast and was keener to learn than Karen. He gave us quite a fright one day when we were out on the lake. He was using a single ski and showing off his recently acquired skills of going out on a whip. He fell off, and it took us a while to get back around to him. We were worried that he was unconscious because he didn't seem to be moving. Fortunately he had only winded himself, but I think he also got a bit of a scare. He was very quiet for the rest of the day and not so keen to do daredevil stunts. Karen was a bit more conservative with her talents and was not as competitive as Matthew.

I was not comfortable with taking the kids out to ski in amongst the high-powered boats because their drivers didn't seem very safety conscious, and I was worried that someone would get hurt. Their skiers would jump from the beach and take off at high speed, irrespective of who might be in their way. To appease my apprehension, we went down to the next lake, where there was less danger. There was no beach from which to do jump starts, and deepwater starts were not as hazardous. I felt much happier when we were down there, but then we had to travel back through the channel between the two lakes, and this was also fraught with danger. We would never ski the kids back through the channel because there was always someone who wanted to pass on the wrong side.

Jim provided us with many hours of entertainment while we had the boat. He would forget to pack the ski ropes, or the skis, or the bait if he was going fishing. There were so many times that we would get to our destination and then find out that a vital piece of equipment had been left behind. It got so bad that the kids drew up two lists headed "Things you need for fishing" and "Things you need for skiing", and they would check off everything required. However, this did not account for other maritime disasters to which Jim seemed to be drawn.

He was out fishing one day with Tom, one of the park residents. Jim had remembered to bring the bait, rods, and tackle, but nobody had thought to put on the list of things he needed "put bungs back in boat". We had a plywood floor in the boat, which meant that at the centre there was about a foot of airspace between the underside of the floor and the hull. Unfortunately, on this occasion he had forgotten to put the bungs in before the boat was launched, and water lapped up over the floor. Scramble stations. Lines reeled in, anchor up, and engine started. The boat was about one-third full of water, and it was therefore very difficult for it to get up on a plane. Tom, who was about thirteen stone, was designated to sit on the nose to try to improve the trim of the boat so that the water would drain out once the boat was moving. Luckily they had plenty of fuel on board because it took quite some time to drain the boat and then insert the bungs to keep it out. This was not the only time that this happened, and it never ceased to amaze us that he could forget something so important to staying afloat!

Bike riding around the park was a popular pastime, and I decided it would help me to get fit. I went to the sporting goods department at David Jones and bought a beautiful maroon Raleigh bicycle, which to my amazement folded up. It was just the thing to fit in the car boot or slide under the annex at Lakeside. Jim was not particularly keen on bike riding since he'd had an accident on his sixteenth birthday. He had collided with a baker's truck and was unconscious for three weeks, so this rather dampened his enthusiasm for bicycles. As we got to know more people in the park, they would want us to stop and chat, so the bike riding became very stop-start. Sometimes it could take half a day just to ride a kilometre.

In the paddock behind us there was a large dam, and each evening a flock of ducks would come in for a splash landing. We could hear them quacking before they were actually visible, and it was very pleasant to watch them swimming in the dam. One summer the dam started to dry up because there had been very little rain. The water level kept dropping, and the ducks were landing on mud with only a few inches of water above it. For the first time we could see the fish that were usually in the bottom of the dam. To help the ducks out, late at night we fitted up our hose to the communal tap and put it through the fence into the pond (unbeknownst to the park owners). We had to make sure that someone got up early each morning to bring the hose back onto our property. It wasn't long before the ducks were splash landing again.

Also in the paddock was Aaron, a sixteen hands palomino stallion. He was beautiful and he knew it. The owner of the farm had other horses, which his children used in gymkhanas, but they were forbidden to ride Aaron because he was too hard to handle. All the caravan blocks along our side of the road backed onto the paddock, and Aaron had developed a "bludge run" for himself. He knew that when we arrived, he would get an apple and some carrots, and he always made sure that he was positioned near our car space to make his presence felt. He would give us no peace with his whinnying and whickering until he had his treat. It wasn't a case of unpacking the car and then feeding the horse. This was not on Aaron's agenda. It was better for our ears if we attended to him first.

Each morning when we stayed at Lakeside, we would be awoken by Aaron making his "feed me" noises about ten feet outside our bedroom window. It was pointless trying to ignore him, but once the window was opened and we acknowledged his presence, he would quiet down for a while—but not for long. Aaron had little patience when he wanted his treat.

One New Year's Eve we had a party in our "backyard", and amongst the food was popcorn. Someone decided to see if Aaron liked popcorn. He did. Someone else thought that some Coca-Cola would be good to wash down the popcorn, and Aaron liked that as well. It was really stupid to give a horse popcorn and Coca-Cola, but he spent all night with his head over our fence as though he was an invited guest. The next day his owner commented that he was being particularly hard to handle, but we played dumb and pretended we didn't know what he was talking about. He would have been quite within his rights to be angry at us for feeding the horse.

The local bowling club was a favourite watering hole each evening. Several of the men had a car pool going and would drive around the park to pick up passengers for happy hour. It was more like "happy many hours" by the time they returned to the park with their dutiful wives waiting impatiently to serve dinner. Friday night was meat raffle night, and quite a contingent would go from the caravan park to try their luck. Those who had cars transported those who didn't. However, the drivers were not always the ones who were sober. The bowling club was located up near the highway, but it was set back off the road and had a side road for access to the car park. This side road was at right angles to the highway and led into the street that completed its length at the gates to the caravan park. If one missed the right-hand turn at the bottom, it was straight down the boat ramp and into the water—which some drivers found out after overindulgence of the amber fluid. It wasn't even safer to walk home because one couldn't be sure who would drive past, hopefully on the correct side of the road. Nobody ever worried about the possibility of the random breath testing units being in one of the side streets, but it would have been a bonanza haul for them any night of the week.

Another social activity at Lakeside was Bingo nights at the barn. Karen, Matthew, and Andrew used to love going to Bingo. One of Andrew's favourite tricks was to hide somewhere in the hall and call out, "Bingo, Merv," which effectively brought the game to a temporary halt while everyone tried to work out who had won. This trick would reduce the three kids to a fit of the giggles, which immediately gave them away. Some of the residents were very serious about their Bingo. Some people would have multicoloured pens to cross off their cards in a contrasting colour or little sloped stands on which to rest their cards, and they always sat at the same table every week. They didn't take kindly to having kids treat the game as a joke.

During our time at Lakeside, the management decided to invest in some daisy carts. They were pedal driven, with two wheels at the back and one at the front, which was connected to a steering wheel. They had a canopy overhead and a seat that would take three people. The day these carts arrived at Lakeside, Karen, Matthew, and Andrew decided to give them a test drive. The son of the park owners and some friends had one cart, and our terrible threesome had another cart. The race was on. They didn't use the roads—they went cross-country through the caravan park, the end result of which was a rolled daisy cart and three kids spilt out onto the grass. They couldn't get up for laughing, and fortunately they were not hurt. Many happy hours were spent in the daisy carts, but by order of management, they were restricted to the roads.

As the years went by and we settled into the Lakeside lifestyle, we invited friends up for weekends, and many of them brought their families up for school holidays. Everybody who borrowed our place looked after it, and some even did improvements while they were there. One of our friends, an electrician, ran wiring from the main caravan across to the annex and installed power points. We were then able to connect an air conditioner, which made hot summer nights more bearable. Again the residents told us we were crazy to go to all this expense, but we felt it was worth it.

We weren't allowed to have pets in the caravan park, and we mostly adhered to this rule—except for one occasion. One Christmas we had invited some friends to use the van, and they were due to arrive as we were leaving to come home. At that particular time our little dog, Charity, had hurt her back, and we had her kennelled at Werriga so that the vet could attend to her if needed. Gemma was kennelled with her to keep her company, and we rang every few days to check that they were okay. We were due to pick them up on our way home, but because of the public holidays, we had to collect the two dogs early in the day and take them back to the park to await our friends' arrival. We smuggled them into the park, hidden under a rug on the back seat. The next trick was to get them from the car to the caravan without them being seen or heard.

I wrapped Gemma up in a beach towel, carried her inside, and went back for Charity. By the time I managed to get Charity into the van, Gemma had her little black nose firmly pressed against the glass doors and was making her presence felt. I tried to keep her quiet, but she wanted to bark and establish her territory. We locked them in the back bedroom and hoped that they wouldn't be discovered before our friends arrived. We had had a barbecue for lunch, and there were eleven sausages left over. I cut a few up for them and put them on a plate. The dogs were so hungry, and the sausages disappeared at a rapid rate. I kept cutting up sausages, and they kept eating them.

Eleven sausages later, they had eaten their fill. I couldn't believe that two little dogs could eat so much, but at least they went and found a sunny spot on the carpet to sleep off their huge lunch.

When our friends arrived, we smuggled the dogs out to the car again and began the journey home. Gemma was becoming more and more agitated as we approached Ryde, and it became obvious from the puddle on the floor that she wanted to go to the toilet. Jim stopped by the side of the road, and the poor little thing must have been at the bursting point. I had never seen a dog wee for so long. She created a mini river that ran down the grass and into the gutter. It took minutes for her to finish, but when she got back into the car, she went straight to sleep and stayed there for the rest of the trip home.

Party Central

J im and I had a pretty good social life for many years with lots of friends, weekends away, and holidays, as well as numerous dinners at our place. We used birthday parties, golf barbecues, anniversaries, and any reason at all for a get-together. Our children were young teenagers, so we tended to invite friends over, and when we got our swimming pool in 1982, our place was dubbed Party Central.

One of our least successful parties was a hungi (or hangi, as the Maoris call it), the instructions for which I found in one of my cookbooks. The idea was to dig a pit, line it with rocks that would heat up with the preliminary fire, wrap a pig or lamb in wire with some device to haul it off the hot coals, and cover with material that would steam, such as wet banana leaves. I thought it was fairly straightforward, so we asked about forty people to come and share the experience.

We dug the pit in the neighbour's backyard because he had more grass than we did, and then we lined it with the bricks Jim brought home from work. They were designed to heat up and retain the temperature, so we thought they would be ideal. Our neighbour, who now had a coffin-shaped pit in his backyard, organised to get us a pig from a butcher friend, and he was to pick it up the day before our hungi. Jim set about burning the covering off some chicken wire for the wrapping, and it was my contribution to peel all the vegetables and wrap them in foil to go in with the pig. I also decided to make some fried rice and salads because I wasn't sure how much meat this pig was going to yield, and I hated to run out of food.

On the day before the hungi, the fire was built in the pit with as much wood as we could find so that the bricks would heat up. The pig was wrapped in the wire with the vegetables, and everything was ready to go. It was supposed to take about six hours to cook, so we decided we would ask our guests to come in the early afternoon for dinner, anticipating that the pig would be cooked as per my cookbook.

We had followed the instructions to the letter, so the pig was extracted from the pit at the appointed time. However, there were no instructions about what to do if it had rained for a week before the pit was to be used, and it was in the lowest, dampest part of the yard. The result: an undercooked, partly steamed pig with half-cooked vegetables and hungry guests. Now was the time for plan B. Jim and a couple of other guys unwrapped the pig and proceeded to slice it up. Some of it was then put on the barbecue, and other bits were hit with a blowtorch. I headed for the house with all the partly cooked vegetables and put them in a hot oven. I also raided the cupboard for extra chips and dips to keep the guests fed until the pig was cooked. It didn't go to plan, but we managed to feed everyone and had a good laugh about our efforts. Oh, and we never did it again!

I was a bit naughty with money if there was something I thought I should have, irrespective of whether Jim agreed with me. In 1989 when Jim was retrenched and we had a bit of spare money, I decided I wanted to buy a car that had power steering and air-conditioning. I told Jim I was going to Westfield to buy some material, but I was actually going to the car yards. I just wanted a small car; a four-cylinder with air-conditioning that was easy on fuel. I knew that Jim would want me to find some gas-guzzler that would take up the length of two car spaces and beat every other car on the road. I found just what I was looking for at the first yard I visited, at $8,500. I put down a $1,500 deposit and arranged an NRMA inspection for the next Monday.

When I got home, Jim asked me why I hadn't bought any material. As I walked away from him, I said in a soft voice, "But I bought a car."

He wasn't sure he had heard right and said, "You bought a *what?*" When I repeated myself, he was not pleased. He wanted to know what sort of a car, what it cost, and where I got the money. When I said that I got the money out of our bank account, he nearly exploded. He wanted to go and see what I had bought, so I took him up to the car yard and showed him the car. As predicted, he didn't like it—it was too small, too expensive, and had too many kilometres. He wanted me to cancel the sale. I didn't want to do that, and after the NRMA inspection found the car to be roadworthy, I took my car on the Monday and traded it in for the one I had chosen. Jim was not the least bit happy about it, but too bad. He had just bought a brand-new van, and I had never had a new car. Jim didn't consider that I had contributed to our financial situation, or the fact that my pre-owned car was only costing about one-quarter of what was being paid for his new van. When he wanted to buy new golf clubs, there was no holding back on the cost. I think he was angrier about the money I had taken out of "our" bank account than the fact I hadn't asked his permission.

We had a lot of fun and many good years together as Karen and Matthew grew up. Karen went to university to do an early childhood teaching degree, and Matthew moved to Melbourne with his mother when he was fourteen; that allowed him to start his flying career. I couldn't get my head around the idea that at nineteen he was an instructor, because it seemed too young to be teaching someone else, but he obviously had the qualifications.

Karen got her driver's licence on her seventeenth birthday and was pleased as punch that she was able to drive—almost as happy as when Matthew failed his on the first attempt.

Emergency—1990

I had had five years of peace from my mother, although I missed my father. In May 1990, my mother started phoning me at home and at work. I couldn't understand why she would do this after five years of not speaking to me or acknowledging my existence; I was suspicious of her motives. The conversations we had skirted the usual forbidden subjects—Jim, Matthew, my job, and my life in general. They mainly focused on what Karen was doing. There was a definite thawing of her hostile attitude to me, but I was still not ready to accept this dubious olive branch. I simply didn't trust her motives.

It was Mum and Dad's birthdays in July, and Mum asked me if Karen and I (no mention of Jim, who was playing golf anyway) would like to go to the Georgetown Motor Boat Club for lunch. I hesitated and then accepted. I was filled with trepidation, wondering what little tricks she would have up her sleeve. I was pleasantly surprised that there was none of her usual tantrums at the lunch, and we parted amicably. That birthday lunch opened the door to more phone calls, but I was not all that sure that they were welcome. Jim and I were happy, and I didn't want the boat rocked again.

For three months I tentatively accepted the phone calls, avoiding the controversial subjects. At the back of my mind sat the thought, *How long is this state of cease-fire going to last?* I always thought of my relationship with my mother in warlike terms.

On Friday, 10 August 1990, I was at work, and for some unknown reason I had a very strong compulsion to go over and have lunch with Mum and Dad. One of our major customers was coming to do a factory inspection, and I couldn't get away until about 1.00 p.m. I rang Mum and asked her, "Would you like a visitor for lunch?"

She replied, "Yes, that would be great." I told her not to worry about keeping something for me to eat because I had my lunch with me, but I would have a cup of tea when I got there. The strong feeling that I had to go over to their house stayed with me all morning. When I arrived, to my surprise my brother was there, too.

Mum poured me a cup of tea, and as the four of us sat around the kitchen table. Dad said, "Isn't this nice, just the four of us?" It was as though someone tipped ice water down my back, and I had a terrible premonition that something catastrophic was about to happen in our lives.

It was 6.00 a.m. on Monday, 13 August 1990, when my bedside phone rang shrilly. Jim was already dressed for work and answered it with his customary cheerfulness. Even in my sleepy state, I realised from the change in his tone of voice that this was not a good-news phone call.

It was my mother. "I can't wake your father," she said in a teary voice. "I could hear him snoring from the other room for hours, and when I went in to try to turn him on his side, he wouldn't wake up."

"I am on my way," I replied, and I hurriedly got dressed to drive over to their house. I didn't know what awaited me, but I knew things were not as they should be. Dad was unconscious and the cause was unknown. The thought went through my head, *At least he isn't dead.*

Mum had phoned her GP, who lived three houses away, and by the time I arrived, some ten minutes after her phone call, the doctor was already there and had called an ambulance. Mum was very upset and apprehensive about Dad's condition; the doctor had given a preliminary diagnosis of either a cerebral haemorrhage or a stroke. Even though we had been given this terrible prognosis, I could not put my arms around my mother and comfort her. The ambulance men lifted Dad onto the stretcher and then had to manoeuvre it along the L-shaped hall, out through the front door and up the driveway into the ambulance. This was no mean feat because Dad was about thirteen and a half stone, and he was unconscious.

I drove my car, and Mum and I followed the ambulance to Western Hospital Emergency Department, where we alternately sat and paced for what seemed like hours. While we waited for word of Dad's condition, I phoned my brother at work. "Charlie, Dad has been taken to Western Hospital, and I am here with Mum at the moment. We don't know whether he has had a stroke or a cerebral haemorrhage, but he is unconscious."

There was a shocked silence on the other end of the phone. When Charlie found his voice again, he said, "Is he okay?"

"I don't know yet, but I will let you know as soon as the doctors tell us something," I replied.

Western Hospital did not have a CAT scan, so they decided to transfer Dad to Bates District Intensive Care Unit for further assessment. Mum was not very happy about this, but she wanted whatever was best for Dad, so it was on to Bates District. I rang my brother again and gave him an update of what was happening. I couldn't get in contact with Jim; as a courier, he spent all day driving. I waited until he got home and rang him there to tell him the news. He wanted to come down to the hospital, but I said, "I'll ring you if things get worse; otherwise, expect me when you see me. It is going to be a long night, so don't worry if I am not home by midnight."

By the time Mum and I arrived at Bates District Hospital, Dad was in the ICU and hooked up to several monitors. He was still unconscious and looked as though he was in a deep sleep. He had the sheet pulled up to his chest and looked too big and healthy to be there, at least compared to the other people in the ward, some of whom had been in car accidents and were badly injured. By late afternoon the waiting room was full of Dad's relatives. Charlie had rung his ex-wife, Leanne, and told her what had happened. She was very fond of Mum and Dad, and even though Charlie and Leanne were divorced, she was still a part of our family. Their daughter Maree and son Trent had come to the hospital with Leanne. I had managed to contact Dad's sister, Evelyn, and she was there with her husband, Jack. Karen had arrived, and Mum and I had been there all day.

We were told Dad had been seen by a neurologist, who came to the waiting room to give his diagnosis and prognosis of Dad's condition. "Mrs. Baker?" he inquired.

"Yes," my mother answered with a shaking voice. "How is he, Doctor?"

The doctor looked at Mum and in a flat, expressionless voice delivered the chilling news. "Your husband has a clot in the brain stem. If he lives—and he may not—he will be a vegetable."

We were stunned. I felt as though I had been hit in the solar plexus with a very large fist, and I could hardly breathe. That big, strong man wasn't going to live? I couldn't take in this news at all; my brain refused to accept what we had been told. The thought that our active, life-loving husband, father, and grandfather was relegated to a life of drip feeds and oblivion—if he lived—was more than we could bear. I secretly wished that he'd die, rather than live like that. Nine pairs of eyes filled with tears, and we looked at each other in stunned silence. Meanwhile the doctor, without another word, went out the door and left us with our private grief and very little hope of Dad ever coming home.

The neurosurgeon on call that night, Dr. Anthony Kwok, visited Dad and painted a slightly more optimistic picture. After more tests, it had been established there was no blood clot in the brain stem, but there was a pool of blood in the brain from the haemorrhage. This had to be drained, which was a very delicate operation and had to be performed as soon as possible. Our spirits lifted that all was not as hopeless as we had been led to believe, but Dad was still a long way from being out of the woods.

He was taken down to theatre, and we were able to wait in the hallway outside the recovery room. To try to lift some of the tension everyone was feeling, Maree and Karen were playing charades and doing a lot of giggling in the process. Aunty Evelyn did not think this was seemly behaviour under the circumstances, but it certainly lightened the atmosphere. Daniel, Karen's boyfriend, arrived after Tech and brought her a Jon Bon Jovi record, *Blaze of Glory*. He knew how much she cared for her pa and was trying to cheer her up.

It was well after midnight before Dr. Kwok came out to tell us the result. He went to a lot of trouble to explain that Dad had had a burst artery in the brain, and that was what had caused the pool of blood. They had stopped the bleeding and had fitted a shunt, which went from the brain down into the abdomen to drain the blood that had collected in the brain; this would allow the brain to resume its normal size. He was to be taken up to ICU, and we could see him for just a few minutes. By then it was 1.00 a.m. We were all so relieved that he was okay so far, but Dr. Kwok made it quite clear that he had a long way to go. His prognosis for Dad's future, based on where the burst artery was located, was that if Dad pulled through, he would have a weakness of the extremities (hands and feet) and some mental confusion possibly affecting his short-term memory. We all felt that was a small price to pay if he lived.

It was too far for Charlie and Leanne and the kids to travel back to Camberville in the early hours of the morning, so Maree came to my place, and the others stayed at Mum's. We didn't anticipate getting much sleep, but we had had a very emotionally exhausting day, and there was nothing else we could do at this stage. Tomorrow was another day.

On Tuesday morning, we all went back to the hospital ICU. The staff would only let one or two of us at a time go in to see Dad, so we took turns. His head was bandaged, he was hooked up to monitors that beeped and recorded his blood pressure and heart rate, and he had an oxygen mask on his face. A sheet covered him from the shoulders down, and he lay motionless in the bed. Only his chest moving up and down, and the monitors, confirmed he was still alive. I don't know whether he could hear us or not, but we spoke quietly to him and told him what we were doing in the outside world. We encouraged him to hang on and keep going. "Don't give up, Dad," I said. "We are all here for you."

Dr. Kwok told us that the shunt monitor was not working properly. Another operation was planned to replace the shunt so that the pool of blood could be reduced. The longer it was left, the less chance of achieving the reduction in the quantity of blood left in the brain. We spent another night outside the recovery room trying to keep up each other's spirits. This time the shunt was working properly, but the blood was not draining away as fast as Dr. Kwok would have liked. That meant another operation to change the shunt over to a smaller size and hopefully reduce the blood pool. Three operations in as many days—Dad must have had the constitution of a horse! Again we waited outside the recovery room until Dr. Kwok could give us an update on his condition.

I was feeling really worn out by Tuesday night, when Dr. Kwok told us that Dad had to have *another* operation. I phoned Jim at home, and he said, "I'll have a shower, get changed, and come down to the hospital."

I have never been so glad to see someone walk along the corridor to meet me. He put his arms around me, and I burst into tears. I couldn't hold them back any longer. "If Dad is going to be a vegetable, I hope he doesn't make it," I said into Jim's shoulder. "I can't imagine him being confined to a bed and having to be fed." It had been an emotionally exhausting forty-eight hours, and I knew it was nowhere near being over.

"I got a taxi down here," Jim informed me. "I didn't think you would be in a fit state to drive your car home." He was absolutely right, and I was so grateful that he had thought to get a taxi.

For eight days, Dad was unconscious and in ICU. The other three people in the ward were there for different reasons. One was a road accident victim who had been in ICU for a month. Some who were in there during the eight days did not make it home, and we felt very lucky that Dad was being transferred out. We still had hope, whereas other families had had their hope wiped out.

When Dad was transferred to a general ward, he still had to be monitored carefully, but we could see a dramatic change in him. The type of haemorrhage he had suffered did not leave him paralysed down one side, but he was mentally confused and had lost a lot of his strength through being unconscious for eight days. During his stay in ICU, he had had physiotherapy on his chest and back to stop him from getting pneumonia, but otherwise he was immobile. He could not even sit up in bed, let alone walk around. He was incontinent, couldn't feed himself, and was unaware that food was on the tray ready to be eaten. He couldn't hold a cup to drink from and had to be fed like a baby. He would cry for no obvious reason. He would say really crude things to the nursing staff, but they understood that he had no control over this.

The father we had had was no longer in existence; he had gone when the artery burst. In his place we had this rather large baby who needed a lot of care and understanding, and that was very hard to deal with. We still didn't know if he would pull through, but each day brought a little more hope. Mum took each day as it came, and she seemed to look to me to monitor how Dad was doing. I didn't resent this, but I couldn't give her the comfort I thought she needed. There were no cosy feelings there, and this tragedy did not erase forty-five years of emotional wilderness.

My mother had lost her partner of forty-nine years. The man she had married no longer existed, and in his place she now had the responsibility of caring for this "replacement husband" who was a complete mystery to her. He was unaware of his surroundings to a great extent and seemed to be in a perpetual state of confusion, which was to be expected after three operations on his brain. He would thrash around in the bed, so he was put in restraints similar to a straight jacket.

We were at a loss of what to do. Dr. Kwok saw Dad regularly over the first few weeks, and occasionally we would be able to speak to him to find out how Dad was progressing. It was a case of "one day at a time"—hopefully in a forward direction. It was obvious that Dad could not feed himself, and the nursing staff was not always available when the food arrived, so the normally unpalatable, lukewarm food became unpalatable, cold food by the time someone could feed him. Sometimes he missed out on his food altogether. The little ethnic ladies would deliver the meal and put it on the tray at the foot of the bed; about an hour or so later, they would return and collect the trays. "You no hungry today?" they would inquire as they deposited the uneaten food back on their trolley. They were obviously unaware that Dad was incapable of feeding himself, and nobody else had had the time to do it for him.

We were a very healthy family and had had very little to do with hospitals and their rituals and rules. One might say we were uninitiated, but we learnt fast. It was obvious that we had to set up some sort of a family roster to make sure that Dad got fed. He had always been one to enjoy his food, and at the moment he was missing a meal here and there, according to the other more alert occupants of the ward. Mum went mid-morning and stayed until late afternoon, making sure he had lunch and some liquids through the day. My shift started at 5.00 p.m. after I finished work, and I fed him his dinner and then went home to attend to my family's meal. Sometimes Karen or Leanne would do the afternoon shift to give me a day off. Weekends were shared amongst us. This became a way of life for us all for sixteen weeks.

When Mum was at home, the phone constantly rang. People were very kind and wanted to know how Dad was doing and whether he was getting better. It was so hard to explain to people what he was like now. We couldn't believe the difference in the father we had had and the one we had now. But he was our Dad, and we loved him and would do whatever we could to get him better and home.

As the weeks went by, it was obvious that he was losing weight. His throat had been so traumatised by the anaesthetic tubes for the three operations that it was almost impossible for him to eat normal food. Feeding Dad was a nightmare. There was a constant fear that he would choke on whatever he was attempting to swallow, so his meal trays frequently went back only half-empty. Liquids were another issue; they seemed to cause more problems to swallow than the food, so they had to be thickened with fruit pulp. Yogurt was one thing that he seemed to be able to swallow more easily, but his food intake was down from what it should have been.

Each day as I approached the hospital, I would wonder what he would be like this time. It was so distressing to see him sitting in a chair beside the bed, strapped in with a restraint and his head lolling to one side. He couldn't read, couldn't concentrate on television (even if he could get to the TV room), and seemed to be unaware of his surroundings. He knew all our names, but he frequently got us mixed up, and it wasn't worth upsetting him to correct his mistakes. We were simply glad he was still alive.

Dr. Kwok had decided that Dad needed another operation and would have to go to Prince Henry to have this done, because it required specialised equipment. He proposed to open up the top of Dad's skull and insert a reservoir so that fluid around the brain could be drawn off, or drugs could be administered. We were alarmed that Dad needed another operation, but we had confidence in Dr. Kwok because he had not given up on getting Dad well enough to come home. And so it was off to Prince Henry. Another night in a waiting room, reading five-year-old magazines with ripped covers, the crosswords completed and the recipes removed. Another night of vinyl lounge chairs and a coffee machine that didn't work. I am sure that if hospital administrators had to spend a night in a waiting room, they would equip them better and not let them be the final resting place for unwanted, mismatched chairs and magazines.

Another successful operation was over. Dad was in a long ward with curtains between the beds, but the care he received was marvellous. He was given a sheepskin rug to lie on, and this was the first inkling we had that Dad had bedsores on his tailbone and his heels. The nursing staff in the neurological ward at Prince Henry were trained to nurse bedridden patients, and their care was superb. In the ten days Dad was there, he was given well-prepared pureed food, most of which he ate, and he seemed to be regaining some of the weight he had lost. Physiotherapy was another feature of the day, and he was also wheeled out onto the covered veranda for some sun.

It was a long drive to Prince Henry after work each day, but Mum and I felt that it was worth every kilometre for the treatment Dad got. After ten days he was transferred back to Bates District. Mum questioned the nursing staff about why he had developed bedsores, and she was told, "Well, you must expect bedsores when someone is in bed for a long time." This was not the view held by the staff at

Prince Henry, and now that we had seen a different way of nursing, we were not satisfied with what was being done.

When Dad was transferred back to Bates District Hospital, Mum asked the staff about getting a sheepskin for him to try to relieve the pressure on his tailbone and the back of his heels. They said that she could buy one if she wanted, but she couldn't blame them if it got lost. Very helpful. Mum went to a shop specialising in equipment for invalids and bought a water cushion across which, in very large and indelible black writing, she wrote Dad's name and telephone number. Hopefully that would bring the cushion back to its rightful owner if it went on a wayward journey. Only time would tell. It certainly seemed to make sitting for long periods more bearable for Dad.

At Prince Henry, all Dad's food was pureed, so we asked the nursing staff at Bates District if they could arrange for the kitchen there to do the same thing because it seemed to be the only way that he was able to swallow. It made the food look even more unappetising than previously. The plate would arrive with four mounds on it: one brown (chicken if it was light, meat if it was dark), one white (potato or rice), one orange (carrots or pumpkin), and one green (broccoli or beans). It was very colourful and probably nutritionally balanced, but that was it—visual appeal did not enter into it. Dessert was another story. If it was white and melting, it was probably ice cream; if it was solid, it was probably custard. Do hospital chefs take a course in how to make normal food look disgusting?

On one occasion in October, Mum went to the hospital to visit Dad, and he wasn't in his bed. She waited for fifteen minutes or so and then discovered that he had been taken down to the shower one and a half hours ago! She immediately went to see the ward sister, and they started a search. Dad, in his hospital gown, had been left down in the bathroom and forgotten. Great! When he came back to the ward, he was shivering with cold; according to Mum, he didn't look very well at all. Not surprising, under the circumstances. The result of this was pneumonia, and he was very ill. It was a real blow to his recovery because every small improvement was welcome, but this set him back.

He was moved to a single ward closer to the nurses station so that his condition could be monitored more easily. Someone forgot to put the sides up on the bed, and he fell out, resulting in a large gash above his left eye. Things were going from bad to worse! His bedsores were getting larger, he now had a gash over his eye, and he was still losing weight. We were beginning to feel that if we didn't get him out of there soon, we would be visiting a brass plaque in a rose garden.

It was a frustrating exercise to try to get any information out of the nursing staff. As soon as we started to ask questions, everyone ran for cover. It was almost impossible to get a doctor to tell us how Dad was progressing, and it was even more difficult to establish when he would be able to go home. We felt as though we were being fobbed off and couldn't get any straight answers.

At the beginning of November, we had a family conference and decided that we should try to bring Dad home. While he was in hospital, he seemed to be deteriorating and appeared to be depressed. When we spoke to the nursing staff about this idea, it was met with very strong opposition, and we were stunned. They didn't think that Mum could look after him at home, and they were of the opinion that he needed twenty-four-hour care. Their idea of "caring" for someone was leaving the patient in a bathroom for one and a half hours. That wouldn't happen if he was at home.

Before they would even consider the idea, we were instructed to see the social worker. Now, she may have been very qualified and a very nice person, but what we got was a whole lot of negatives about bringing Dad home. I will be the first to admit that the idea of a seventy-year-old lady looking after a seventy-two-year-old man is not unheard of, but my mother is only four feet ten inches, and my father is five feet ten and of a much heavier build. What was disregarded by the social worker was the fact that it was *what my mother wanted to do*. Mum wasn't being coerced into it by the family; it was entirely her decision that she wanted to at least give it a try, and we were all prepared to help out wherever we could. The social worker tried everything she could to talk Mum into putting Dad into a nursing home. This was like a red rag to a bull, and Mum really lost her temper. "What right do you have to tell me what I should do about my husband?" she raged. "We have been married for forty-nine years, and I think I should know better than anyone what he is like."

The social worker backed down a bit but insisted on Mum taking a list of nursing home names and at least putting Dad's name down, "just in case". Well, the list didn't make it past the first bin outside the building. Doreen was in full sail, and she was taking Dad home as soon as possible. When we went back to the ward and told them about the interview with the social worker, they again reiterated that Dad required twenty-four-hour care. They suggested that Mum take him home one weekend on trial, to see how she coped, with the proviso that we go to the hospital for a day and see what had to be done for him. We agreed.

I took a day off work, and Mum and I duly reported for "nursing duty" at 8.00 a.m. as instructed. Dad was still in bed and had not finished his breakfast. Nobody came near him until 9.30 a.m., and that was to change his bed. He was then helped to the chair beside the bed with a rug tucked around his knees, and they left him until 11.00 a.m. So far, Mum and I had seen nothing to suggest that this amount of activity could not be performed adequately at home. We did realise that some assistance would be required from home nursing for showers and dressing Dad's bedsores.

At 11.30 a.m. Dad, Mum, and I went down to the rehabilitation department to learn how to move Dad from the bed to a chair and vice versa. We were given instructions on how to help him to walk in a frame, which the physiotherapists had started a few weeks before, and how to lift him. After a few hours down in rehab, we felt confident that bringing Dad home and caring for him was not an insurmountable problem. It was going to take a certain amount of input from everyone, but we felt that it could be done.

When Dad was admitted to hospital, he had been catheterised, and this was still in place. He was wearing a leg bag the day we went down to rehabilitation, and the smell of his urine was pure ammonia. On our return to the ward, after our trip down to rehab, we mentioned this to the nursing staff. "That is quite normal," we were told, but we were not convinced.

The next time we saw a doctor in the ward, we asked them the same thing. "It could be a slight infection. We will put him on some antibiotics," he said. So much for it being "normal". We were fast losing what little confidence we had in the staff.

The head nursing sister on the ward finally but reluctantly agreed that we could take Dad home for a weekend trial. We had fulfilled all their requests of seeing the social worker and having the day of "training" at the hospital, and there was nothing else they could do. It was my birthday the next weekend, so we made arrangements to bring Dad home from Saturday morning to Sunday afternoon. The nursing sister was still of the opinion that after a weekend at home, we would want to consider nursing home options, and she inquired if we had put Dad's name down on some lists. Mum assured her that we had, just to keep her quiet. No way was Mum going to have anything to do with nursing homes if she could possibly help it. The experience of her mother being in a few nursing homes at the end of her days was vivid in my mother's memory, especially the smell of urine.

Saturday morning arrived, and at 10.00 a.m. we duly presented ourselves at the hospital. Dad was sitting in the chair beside his bed, and Mum busied herself with packing some of his things so that he could come home. We had to get some medication and other instructions before we signed the papers, and by 11.00 a.m. we were on our way. We had to take Dad in a wheelchair from the ward to the lift and then down all the corridors of the ground floor. The hardest part was getting Dad from the wheelchair into the car because there was no cutaway in the gutter to get him close to the door. Fortunately there was a very nice man visiting his father, and he helped us with Dad.

We had a folding walking frame and a wheelchair on loan for the weekend, and we finally managed to work out the mechanics of these two aids to get them both in the boot. Where there was a will, there was a way. Home, here we came! We pulled into the driveway at Mum's house full of optimism for this weekend that would be the start of Dad returning to his home. This optimism was soon depleted.

We unloaded the wheelchair and assembled it, but we decided to forgo the walking frame because we were not too sure how good Dad was at managing it. We wheeled Dad from the car to the bottom of the two steps which went up to the veranda, a distance of about fifteen feet; the distance from the steps to the front door was about the same. Mum and I helped Dad up the two steps, and he very shakily stood on the top step ready for the walk across the veranda. Mum was on one side of him, and I was on the other. He had lost a lot of weight, and even though he now only weighed about ten stone, all that weight was pressing down on our shoulders. Mum fared the worst because she was shorter. It took us thirty minutes to get him across the veranda, one shuffle at a time. One of us couldn't leave and get the wheelchair, because the other wouldn't be able to hold him up. We were all exhausted by the time we got into the house. There was a recliner chair just inside the lounge room and close to the front door, and we very unceremoniously dumped Dad into it because we couldn't hold him up anymore. Mum and I were a lather of perspiration, and Dad was white from the effort of walking that short distance. Suddenly this weekend did not seem to be such a good idea.

We were not quitters and were optimistic that somehow we could make this work. It may require some extra equipment and a little more manpower (or in our case womanpower), but we would give it our best shot. After the veranda marathon, a cup of tea was definitely in order and was thoroughly enjoyed by everyone. Dad's throat had still not recovered, and he had difficulty with liquids, often to the point of almost choking. Hopefully this would get better with time. The trial weekend had started, and so far we had survived two hours.

The next problem was the trip down the hall and into the bedroom, but we decided to achieve this by wheeling him. The hall was L-shaped and had a glass half table right in the corner. This had to go or else it would be wiped out by the wheelchair, so we set about disassembling it and packing it away. Getting Dad into bed was not as difficult as we thought it was going to be, but he was so weak that he couldn't lift himself up or turn over. This was not something that we had been aware of, and again we had to work out a solution. Extra pillows were put under his back so that he could lie on one side for a while and stay off the bedsore on his tailbone; it also meant that his heels would not have pressure on them. Up to this stage we had only heard about the bedsores but had never actually having seen them, because there was always a dressing over them.

Dad was very tired and slept for most of the day, but he seemed pleased to be in his own home. He still was not very communicative and got confused about the day or time or person, but that didn't matter to us and didn't seem to distress him unduly. If this was the father we were going to have from now on, then we had to make the most of it. He had been so close to death that we were lucky to have a father at all. It was a great birthday present for me to have my father come home after sixteen weeks in the hospital, and we all hoped that this weekend would work out and that this would be a permanent arrangement.

We got through the weekend quite successfully, we thought, and we took Dad back on the Sunday afternoon at the agreed time. "Well, how did you do?" the nursing staff asked.

"Great," said Mum. "No problems at all. Now, when can he come home permanently?" She was never one to waste words—direct-approach Doreen. After much discussion with the nursing staff about what support equipment and services were required for Dad to be at home permanently, it was agreed that he could come home on Tuesday. Great news!

On Tuesday we once again presented ourselves at the hospital and were advised that an appointment had been made for Dad to go and see Dr. Kwok in a few weeks' time, at Bankstown. When Dad was in his most confused state, he called Dr. Kwok "Kwok-a-doodle-doo", but the doctor didn't seem upset by this. I guess when you are a neurosurgeon, this type of behaviour comes with the job. Mum headed straight for Dad's locker and started throwing everything into a bag as though she was afraid that if it wasn't all packed in ten minutes flat, they would repossess him. The papers for his discharge weren't ready and took forever to complete, or it seemed so to us. We were given last-minute instructions on how to puree his food, and we received some blood pressure tablets and antibiotics. Admittedly we were impatient, but after sixteen and a half weeks and the ups and downs of his recovery, we were glad he was fit enough to come home. At last we were getting out of there—permanently, we hoped.

Dad was pale, confused, incontinent, and hardly able to walk, but he was ours, and he was going home. We had seen many people throughout that time who did not make it home, or to any other destination than the morgue. One of the saddest cases was the father of the nice man who helped us get Dad into the car the previous Saturday. His father was dying of cancer and was obviously in great pain, even with medical intervention. We could hear him moaning or gasping for breath, and it must have been a terrible way to die; it was certainly dreadful for his family to watch.

Once more we went through the labyrinth of corridors and out into the street. This time we were smarter and parked in a different place with a cutaway edge. We were getting to be old hands with this wheelchair and had it stowed in the boot in no time at all. This time when we got home, we wheeled Dad into the house. We didn't make the same mistake twice by trying to walk him across the veranda.

Home sweet home. It was now a case of how best to manage Dad's care between us all and work out what was required and what could be done by whom. One problem was that Dad not being able to turn over in bed, so we decided that it might be better if he spent all day out of bed, sitting in a chair on his water cushion. This should help the bedsore on the base of his spine, and it would also stop him rubbing his heels up and down the sheets, irritating those bedsores as well. He still had a leg bag on for the urine but would need to go on the commode for anything else; this was something that would have to be worked out as we went along. The home nursing sisters were to come each day and shower Dad and change the dressings on the bedsore. He needed a stool in the shower because he was not strong enough to stand for more than a minute, and this item was provided on a temporary basis by the CRAGS unit at the hospital. If Dad was staying at home, we were advised to contact the Veterans Affairs department, and they would bring the equipment and also arrange for crash bars in the bathroom near the toilet and in the shower.

Within days of being home, Dad started to be able to eat things that were not pureed. We came to the conclusion much later that the trauma of the throat tubes during the operations and the long stay in hospital contributed to the problem of not being able to swallow properly. It was as though his throat had gone into spasms, and when he came home and relaxed, his swallowing mechanism returned to normal. It was great to see him able to eat normal food again.

Our spirits lifted with every day that he was still with us and improving all the time. It was hard work, particularly for Mum. There was a constant stream of well-meaning visitors, and the phone never stopped. This was very time consuming, and it meant that Mum wasn't getting much rest and was becoming tired. She wasn't sleeping properly, and if Dad snored, she was once again transported back to the night he had had the cerebral haemorrhage, so she would get up and go in to make sure he was all right. After a few days and nights of this, she was exhausted but was not prepared to give up. She wanted to look after Dad at home, and by golly, she was going to give it her best shot.

We decided that if I came over in the morning before I went to work, I could give her a hand with Dad to get him out of bed and into his chair. He was still very weak and couldn't help much while we tried to sit him up. I climbed on the bed on one side of him, and Mum was on the other side. "On the count of three, lift him up under the arms," I said. He was a dead weight, and it took a few attempts before we achieved our goal. Once he was actually sitting up, it was then a matter of Mum swinging his legs over the side of the bed while I kept him in an upright position. When his legs were pointing towards the floor, we brought the wheelchair closer to the bed, let the side of the chair down, and pushed and shoved Dad into it. About this time I think we were grateful he was now only ten stone and not his original thirteen and a half. I don't think we would have managed if he had been.

While there, I could help give Dad his breakfast, which gave Mum a chance to do a load of washing and get it out on the line. The phone calls from caring people started early in the morning and continued on throughout the day. She needed an answering machine so that nobody's call was missed, if we couldn't get to the phone right at that moment. It helped enormously and meant that Mum could at least have a meal in peace or take a well-earned, ten-minute tea break without having to answer the phone.

None of us had ever been in a similar situation before, except my Aunty Evelyn. Her husband, Jack, had been hit by a car one night when he had been crossing the road near their home, and he had suffered a fractured skull. He was left with some brain damage but seemed to be improving a little each day, although he would never be what he used to be. Aunty Evelyn would ring most days and offer all sorts of advice about what we should do. Mum and she had never been really good friends, so her advice was usually ignored, but one had to give points for persistence. What we needed was hands-on assistance, not advice via Telecom.

Celia and Ron, who used to live in Mum and Dad's flat in the backyard, now lived at Ulara. They came down every week or fortnight, whenever they could spare the time, and they would massage Dad's arms and legs and help in any way they could. Celia worked in the dementia ward of their local hospital and was used to handling people with brain damage. Her advice was invaluable, and she gave us many pointers on how to manage. Ron knew a fair bit about massage, which was also helpful to Dad.

We battled on with the help of the home nursing service, which provided assistance with daily showers and dressing of the slowly healing bedsores. On their first visit, the nurses were horrified at the depth of the sores and mentioned that one of the sores was on its way to becoming gangrene. Dad was very fortunate that he had good circulation, or his recovery from the bedsores would not have been so successful.

An appointment had been made with Dr. Kwok to take Dad back for a checkup about a month after he was discharged from hospital. I drove Mum and Dad over to Bankstown, and Karen was also with us. We had a flat tyre along Kings Road and pulled into a service station to ask if they would change the tyre for us. No chance—they only serve petrol! Fortunately Karen knew how to perform this task, so we got Dad out of the car and helped him to stand, leaning on the side door, while Karen changed the tyre. Not one male worker came over to offer help, but I guess that is the price one pays for "equality".

We finally made it to Bankstown and had trouble parking near the doctor's surgery. Eventually we made the decision that we would double-park to get Dad out of the car, and then I would take the car and park it somewhere. So far, so good. Dad was very shaky on his legs, but we made it up the ramp and into the foyer of the building, and we felt pretty pleased with ourselves. We asked the reception desk where Dr. Kwok's room was, and the receptionist pointed towards the heavens, to be reached by a wide stairway. I made the comment, "What would possess a neurosurgeon to have his rooms on the first floor? How ridiculous." When I turned around to see where we had to go, Dr. Kwok was looking over the rail at me. I was a bit embarrassed to say the least, but I still thought that a first-floor room for a specialist treating people with brain injuries was a bit stupid. We then found out we could have taken him to Bondi Junction where there was a lift, but nobody thought to give us that option at the time of making the appointment.

We pushed, pulled, and tugged Dad up that flight of stairs, and all of us were about ready to collapse by the time we got to the top. We manoeuvred Dad to the waiting room and went into the doctor's room straight away because Dad was the first patient for the morning. Dr. Kwok said that he didn't think Dad would make it this far into his recovery, but he hadn't counted on Dad's strength and Mum's determination.

The descent of the stairs was more terrifying than the ascent. We were really frightened that if he tumbled forward, we would not be able to stop him. It took the combined teamwork of Karen and I on each side of Dad, and Mum hanging onto his belt like a rear brake, to get him to the ground floor. All that for a fifteen-minute consultation!

Some weeks after his discharge from Bates District, Dad had to go back to the hospital to have the catheter changed. He arrived by ambulance transport, and he was to be taken back home after the procedure was completed. Dad was left sitting in a wheelchair in the waiting room, and he decided that the ambulance was taking too long to come back and get him. Never one to sit around and wait for things to happen, he got out of the wheelchair and somehow made it to the sliding glass entry doors. The driveway going past the doors was sloped, and Dad started to lose his balance and eventually fell over. The staff from the hospital came out, put Dad back into the wheelchair, and took him back into the accident and emergency department. They apparently gave him a cursory examination and then sent him home.

He had been home for only a few hours, and it was obvious to Mum that he was in pain and had some problem with his hip. Mum had been told by the ambulance people that Dad had "had a bit of a fall but was okay". Mum rang the doctor, and when he came, he offered the opinion that he thought Dad had a broken hip and should go back to hospital. An ambulance was called, and for the second time that day Dad was back in Bates District Hospital. This time they X-rayed him and confirmed that his hip was broken and would need a pin to repair it.

We had to wait several hours for an orthopaedic surgeon to be available, and it was well into the early hours of the morning before Dad got his operation. He spent about a week in Bates District, and we were advised that he should go to Lady Davidson Hospital at Turramurra for rehabilitation. Dad was transferred by ambulance, and Mum was concerned about whether he would be looked after properly, but after visiting him there she was satisfied that he was in good hands.

They had Dad up and walking in a few days, and he was managing quite well with the walking frame—so well that he escaped. He presented himself at administration and said he wanted to go home. They thought they had placated him with promises of, "Yes, Mr. Baker, in a few days." Not good enough for the impatient Alf. He took himself up almost to the main road before someone saw him and brought him back to the hospital. He told Mum he was going to get a bus and come home! Unfortunately, he missed his granddaughter's twenty-first birthday while in hospital.

While Dad was in Lady Davidson Hospital, I finished work at 3.00 p.m. a few days a week and took Mum up to Turramurra. It became part of the weekly routine to build in a drive to the hospital a few afternoons each week. My boss was absolutely marvellous about letting me go early, and I really appreciated his compassion.

When Jim finished work each afternoon, he usually came over and helped Dad walk in a frame around the house, except for Thursdays because that was Jim's snooker night. As the weeks and then months went by, Jim got Dad to walk up the driveway, and then they ventured further afield with Jim hanging onto Dad's arm. It was a family joke that Dad told everyone he had a five-foot rod in his leg. If that had been the case, it would have been sticking out of his shoulder.

Dad eventually came home, and within only a few days he had another fall in the lounge room. This time he sliced his ear open on a sharp edge of the coffee table, and the local doctor had to stitch it at home. Throughout all these months of drama and trauma, my mother mostly remained calm, dealt with each blow as it came, and simply got on with her new life.

I missed not having the father who built houses on hills, spray-painted cars, went fishing, and could go wherever and do whatever he wanted. He had left sometime in the early hours of 13 August 1990 and wasn't coming back.

Life Goes On

Karen still lived with us and often brought the boy of the week home for meals. Some of the boys we liked and some we didn't, but that was the way of things. When she brought home John, now my son-in-law, I liked him on sight and hoped he would be a keeper.

Karen continued to see her father on weekends, and Matthew flew from wherever he was living at the time to visit us. Alternatively, we would take a flight to stay with him for a few days. We certainly got to see a fair bit of the capital cities of Australia while he was trying to find a permanent position with an airline

Karen rang me about seven o'clock one August night in 1997 from her father's place; she had taken the car up there because it needed some work. The garage door was slightly open, the dog was in the garage, and the house was in darkness. She was really concerned, so I went up there to see what was happening. It felt very strange to go back into my ex-husband's house, where I had lived with him and my mother-in-law back in 1970. I put the lights on and could see David lying on the bed, not moving. I feared the worst and was right: he had passed away some time that afternoon.

My daughter was inconsolable. Her beloved dad had died at only fifty-five years of age. He had had a heart condition that required bypass surgery when he was forty-two, and again when he was about fifty-three, but he hadn't made it to his third operation, which might have saved his life. I rang the police and explained the situation, and they arrived about an hour later. They were marvellous with Karen and said she should go in and say good-bye to her dad while he was still in the house. She rang John, and he was there within what seemed minutes.

It was a very sad time for Karen because she had no siblings to help her with the funeral arrangements, and I was certainly not welcome in the scheme of things. John was her rock and helped her get through what was an awful time in her young life.

Karen and John continued to go out together and bought a house between them, which John lived in until their marriage in early 2000, and then Karen moved in. It was a happy time in the family, preparing for the wedding, and Dad was able to be there after a lot of physiotherapy by my friend Colleen. I don't think he would have missed his granddaughter's wedding if he had to crawl there. He was going steadily downhill as he got older, but he managed to get to the wedding with a lot of help from friends and family, and apart from having a little nap in the middle of the reception, he was there for all of it.

When Karen's dad passed away, his will gave her the property at Kennedy Bay, the house I had lived in with him and his mother some twenty-five years before. However, there was a phrase in the will that gave David's sister the use of the property provided that she keep up the maintenance and pay all the bills for the house. After a lot of legal letters between the solicitors over two years, Karen obtained clear title to the property.

Karen and John were married by the time the legal battles were resolved, and their son, Cameron, arrived in 2001 just three months after my father passed away. They decided to renovate the house because the one they had purchased together was small and had limited renovation potential. The house Karen inherited was much larger and could be extended, but it was built in 1965 for a little, grey-haired old lady and her son, so only two bedrooms were required. It was certainly not big enough for a growing family.

They drew up plans for renovations, carried out the work, sold the smaller home, and moved in to a two-storey home with plenty of room for everyone. It is a lovely home, built on the foundations that were going to be a dungeon flat for David and I back in 1969. I can visit there with no fear of a dumpy, little old lady telling me I can't come in. Karma is a funny thing.

In 2004 Jade was born, and I then had a grandson and granddaughter. Over the following years I looked after both my grandchildren, prior to them going to preschool and starting school. It was a wonderful time, and we had lots of fun with visits to the library every Wednesday morning and then a café for morning tea. As they got older, we had grandma dates on weekends or school holidays, but they were very different in their preferences, though they usually agreed on which movie to see.

When Dad was approaching the end of his life and was being totally cared for by Mum, I did not feel guilty about not wanting to, or being able to, stand up for him against her. He hadn't stood up for my brother and me, when we were children and unable to defend ourselves against her moods and temper tantrums. He had created this monster that could do whatever she liked towards those in her "care", because nobody had ever told her it was wrong. We even have on Karen's wedding video Mum giving Dad a slap across the shoulder when he was eating, probably because he had spilt something on his clothes. That was one time she let down her street angel persona, and we even have it on film.

My brother hadn't seen Dad since 1996, when he and Mum had had an argument on the front veranda one Mother's Day. Charlie was supposed to look after Dad while Mum, Karen, and I went out to lunch. When he walked down the driveway, his body language showed displeasure: he had a frown and hunched shoulders—he obviously didn't want to be there.

Mum asked him how his son Trent was, and he replied that Maree (his daughter) was good, too. Mum told him that she didn't give a shit about how Maree was. Charlie told her to apologise, or he wouldn't be coming back. She didn't apologise, and he never went back, except for just before Dad died, and it certainly wasn't to see Mum.

We knew Dad was down to the last week or so of his life because he wasn't eating or drinking, and he was in a semi-coma for most of the day. With Mum's permission given reluctantly, I arranged to contact Charlie and let him know so that he could come and see Dad before it was too late. It was Thursday night, so Mum and I went to a local shopping centre, and Trent, Maree, Charlie, and his ex-wife Leanne came down in the early evening to see Dad. We had arranged that Charlie would text me when they were leaving so that Mum and I could go home.

The next morning I packed a bag and planned to stay at Mum's until Dad passed away, which we anticipated would only be a few days, according to the doctor. Dad was in and out of consciousness, and in one of his more lucid moments he looked straight at me and said, "I wish I had stood up for you more." I reassured him that he had been a good dad and he should not to worry about the past. He had had a taste of being cared for by Mum for eleven years, and I think he understood just how difficult she could be.

During that long weekend, I suggested to Mum that we get ourselves organised for the eventual end of Dad's life. The order of service was done, flowers were ordered with delivery date unknown, and a rough draft of the funeral notice was drawn up. I asked Mum to get Dad's clothes ready and find whatever paperwork was required; then we could make up a list of names and telephone number of people she would like notified. It kept her busy, and I knew she wouldn't be capable of doing this later.

On Monday afternoon my friend Fay and I went to the local shops for a coffee and a break from the phone calls. We were only gone thirty minutes, and when we returned I could hear Mum's shoes tapping up the hallway. She flung the door open and shouted at me, "He just died. You left me alone!" Did I ever get anything right?

It was then my job to contact the funeral home, and they arrived after dark. I took them down the hall to Dad's room and then went back to the front of the house. Mum and Fay were in the kitchen with the doors closed, because Mum couldn't deal with Dad being taken away. I will never forget the sound of the zips on the bag just before they loaded Dad on the trolley to take him away.

Dad passed away on 25 June 2001. Karen was six months pregnant with her first child and my first grandchild. Karen's pregnancy was a bright spot in an otherwise bleak time of our lives. She had lost her dad a few years before, and now her beloved Pa.

My brother and his family sat at the back of the chapel, because he didn't want to be anywhere near Mum. It was commented on why they hadn't sat in the family pew at the front, but not a lot of people knew what had gone on between Charlie and Mum, and she was not about to enlighten them. It would not have been in her best interests.

Cameron arrived at 7.07 a.m. on 15 September 2001, and Karen and I had the most confusing conversation. She was supposed to have a Caesarean section early the next week, but Cameron apparently wasn't advised of this plan. Karen rang me at nine on the Saturday morning Cameron was born and said, "I've got a baby." She had been having dreams about babies and names, and I thought it was just another dream.

I said, "Oh, that's good, what's this one?" She replied, "No, I really have a baby. He is here with me now." Then I heard him cry. Well, that woke me up. She was a bit disappointed that I wasn't more excited, because I had so looked forward to the arrival of my first grandchild. I was confused because I thought she was telling me about another dream. We got it sorted eventually, and Jim and I stopped by Karen's house, because she had gone into the hospital in the middle of the night; I collected what she had asked me to get for her. In the meantime John had rung Mum and told her the news, so she expected me to be at her doorstep immediately. I knew nothing about all this and went to the hospital to see my new little grandson, whom I fell in love with at first sight.

When I was outside the hospital and on my way home to drop Jim off, I was able to use my mobile phone, and all that was on my voicemail was Mum screaming and trying to find out where I was. I didn't bother to reply because I was almost to her place by the time all the messages played, so I just pulled up in the driveway. She was in quite a temper. She had a bunch of flowers in her hand, and before I had taken two steps towards the house, she yelled across the driveway, "I am so disappointed. A bloody boy." I almost burst into tears. This was my first grandchild, her first great-grandchild, and she was complaining that it was a boy. "If you don't want to see him, you don't have to," I said, and I went to get back in the car. Of course she changed her mind, because what would the neighbours think?

While Karen was in hospital, Mum expected me to take her there every time I went, but I wanted time with my daughter, and Karen needed time with John and her new son. There were several times that I sneaked to the hospital without Mum knowing I had been there. It was easier for me to lie about where I had been. Karen arrived home from hospital five days later, and I really enjoyed going to her place and helping care for Cameron. I took him out for a walk in the pram so Karen could catch up on some sleep or chores, and I got to know this special little person. It certainly gave our family another new dimension.

In December 2001, when Cameron was three months old, Matthew and Bonita got married in Canberra. Jim and I helped with their wedding plans and all the other things that parents do for their children. We gave them the same amount of money that Karen's wedding had cost, because we were always fair about what we spent on each of our children. Some of Bonita's family came out from South America, and when the wedding was over, they stayed in our house in Sydney for a week; we went to stay with friends in Queensland. This was another bright spot in 2001, and the second half of that year was certainly better than the first half.

Running-Away Account

I was only fifty when I was diagnosed with depression—at the same time that I began menopause, which was a double whammy for any female. I wasn't really sure for a while which of my symptoms and feelings belonged to depression, and how much should be attributed to the end of my childbearing years. It took a while for my general practitioner to unravel what was what, and I then started the appropriate medication.

Along with the medication for depression, I was advised to see a psychologist because I had a lot of deep-running issues about my mother that needed to be resolved. I spent a few thousand dollars and about eighteen months working through my stuff, and then I had to discontinue treatment because I could no longer afford the fees. In 1994 Medicare did not support rebates for psychology consultations, but fortunately now it is possible to access this service with referrals from my GP. I learned a lot about myself, and how I reacted to having my mother push my emotional buttons. Mothers and daughters often have this weird dance where they know what will set the other off, and just how hard to step on the other person's toes.

My mother and I had never really gotten along, and when I was a teenager and she was only thirty-seven, she started the "change of life", as it used to be called; she had regular doses of hormones and behaved erratically for the majority of every month. With this in my background, I was rather anxious about how I would react to menopause, and I hoped that it would be an easier journey for me than it had been for her. My daughter still refers to it as "You remember when", but mostly I don't because I was in some sort of hormonal fog most of the time. If you have been through it or know people who have, you will appreciate the look of desperation that comes over their face when they realise they don't know where their car is in a massive shopping centre car park; ask them what sort of car or number plate, and it is almost as though they have been struck down by lightning. Instead of putting the milk in the fridge, I put the keys there, I looked for sunglasses, which were already on my face, and I wore two different shoes to work, although both were black.

These were only some of the less harmful things I did. Sometimes I used to hear my mouth saying things my brain hadn't even thought of, such as the night Jim and I were in a restaurant, and I blurted out to all and sundry that his mother was a space waste. Stunned silence didn't even touch the edges of the effect that statement had on my dinner companions.

The hot flushes, night sweats, or whatever else they are called were very debilitating in lots of ways. Try spending all night throwing off the blankets, only to reach down twenty minutes later to retrieve them from the floor. Sleep deprivation was terrible, and the next day was a battle.

It also affected one's sex life, if that was still on the agenda, although it was assuming less and less importance on mine, I was unaware that this was a side effect of the medication that nobody had thought to mention. The physical effects of decreasing hormones were bad enough, but the mood swings were horrendous. Add into the mix a husband who was never ill for any reason, other than from drinking too much, and menopause was a very lonely path to tread. It was debilitating in so many ways, and few people understood what it was like for the woman experiencing it. I wrote a poem while I was in the grip of menopause, at age fifty-five.

Sunflowers
13/8/99

Sparkling clear dewdrops hold on tight,
Dropped onto the petals throughout the night.
The sunflower centre stubbly and round,
Golden velvet petals soft as duck down.
Each petal named with a thing I do,
The many facets of what I am, and who.
Creativity, craft, and love of life;
A mother, daughter, friend, and wife:
I was all these things and many more—
Till the bleakness of depression sneaked in the door.

Unaware of it happening till nearly too late,
One day I awoke, and it was already eight,
Not keen to arise, pulled the blankets back up,
Closed my eyes again, curled up like a pup.
No desire to start my day,
Wished the world would just drift away.
Lost all the joy in my very busy life,
Even lost interest in being a wife.
No friends invited for dinner, no outings
arranged in advance,
No desire to do any gardening,
Even less reason to go out and dance.
My petals of life, slowly one by one,
Withered and died, until there were none,
All that was left was dull and brown,
The death of the petals made not a sound.
I knew I needed help on a morning so bleak,
I was dispirited, unhappy, too tired to speak.
Couldn't care less if the day never finished,
Only I knew how far life had diminished.
The road to recovery is not easy, my friend,
Much work by professionals before the end.
Soul-searching, changes, and help along the way,
All leading to return to a sunny day.
The petals started growing again, one by one,
Turning their golden faces towards the sun.
My life has started to turn around,
Positive thoughts and hope abound.
The petals keep growing, and soon there will be
A happy and healthy return to "me".

I gradually clawed my way back to what had been my life, but unfortunately I wasn't able to take my marriage on the journey to recovery. I no longer had any interest in going to the same old places, seeing the same people, and talking the same talk. I was bored, was lonely, and had no idea of what I was going to do with the rest of my life, but I was coming to the conclusion that this life I had was going to be changed, discarded, or in some way made better. I didn't know how I was going to manage it, so I started up my running-away account.

Since her marriage, I missed my daughter's companionship quite a lot, because we had spent time going to the gym for an early morning class or walking on weekends, and I could usually rely on her to go on a girls-only shopping expedition. I never thought I would suffer from the empty-nest syndrome, but being at home with just my husband for company became quite difficult. We really didn't have much to say to each other after twenty-two years, which was quite sad.

I had been going out with friends for company, because Jim wasn't interested in the same things as me anymore. I had asked him to go to musicals, plays, and symphonies, but the standard reply was, "I am not interested." I tried to schedule my outings for times I knew he would be home watching football on television, generally Friday and Saturday nights, so that we could still have some time together on the weekend. It wasn't long before I realised that this marriage was headed for the scrap heap, and I had to work out what I was going to do if I didn't want to spend the rest of my life sitting on a couch in the lounge room and watching Jim sleep every night.

It turned out that 2001 was quite a tumultuous year in our family. In June my father passed away, Jim needed shoulder surgery from a work accident in July, my first grandchild Cameron was born by Caesarean in September, and my stepson married in December. I also decided to take a year off work because everybody seemed to need my help, and I couldn't spread myself around enough.

I did a lot of thinking in the next two years about the state of my marriage. I realised that the time was approaching when I had to make a decision on what I wanted for the rest of my life. It really came down to stay, or go, and the latter won.

Jim and I were living in the home he had shared with his first wife and his son, and Matthew often mentioned that it was his father's house. That was certainly true, but it annoyed me nonetheless, so when we bought an investment property in the 1980s, my name was added to the title of our marital home. At least that would ensure I got a fair share—not like my first marriage, when I walked away with no financial settlement at all.

When I was sure that I didn't want to be in my second marriage anymore, a friend of mine advised me to start up a running-away account. I knew for an absolute fact that my husband would not be the one moving out, and therefore it would be me, so I had to get some dollars together. I am not usually a sneaky person, but my husband and I had joint bank accounts, and he would of course be curious if he saw an envelope arrive from a bank with just my name in the window. I didn't have a bank account of my own, which was a big mistake in hindsight. It would be very difficult to explain a new account, so to avoid this possibility I opened an account in my name but at my daughter's address, with her permission.

I had calculated that I would need in excess of five thousand dollars to re-establish myself by the time I paid a rental bond, had utilities connected, and bought some new furniture. I didn't particularly want to take any of our furniture because I wanted a fresh start and didn't want to be constantly reminded of from what I was walking away. I was more upset about having to leave my pets behind than leaving my husband.

I had no money of my own invested, and this was also a big mistake. All married people, whether male or female, should have some dollars put aside for a rainy day. Over the time I was married, I had contributed to the household budget, but there never seemed enough for me to put some aside—and to be fair, I didn't foresee that I would need access to some cash of my own to change my life. However, things had changed and saving hard was required.

The major amount of our combined assets was in a superannuation fund, which I had no right to use while I was still married to Jim, as far as the law was concerned. We earned our money, paid the bills, and had a good time with what was left over. Holidays were an annual occurrence, and weekends away to go into the city and see a show were put on the credit card and then paid for when the next statement arrived. Having a household budget was not one of our strong points, and we tended to live by the idea of "have it today, spend it today, and worry about it tomorrow".

I knew that when I was ready to leave my second marriage, I would have to support myself financially, because never again would I be held to ransom over some money, as I was by my first husband. I wanted complete control over my life, and I fought to get it, even though my husband and mother had different ideas about what my future life should be.

I knew I could save money from my part-time job, and my daughter gave me fifty dollars per day to mind the grandchildren, so it was not difficult to gradually put some money aside. I cut down on the amount of groceries that I bought, stretched out the time between haircuts, didn't spend so much on gifts for people outside the family, and gradually started to build up my savings. Every dollar I squirreled away was another dollar closer to escaping from this life that I wanted so desperately to leave.

To Jim, his superannuation account was sacrosanct, and he saw it as his retirement money on which he—note that I was not included—would live. He looked on this money as being entirely his own and was of the opinion, rightly or wrongly, that I had no right to it. However, when it came to dividing up our assets, it was very much taken into account by law, and he was not at all happy about it. After being married to Jim for such a long time, I knew that he would resist moving out of the house and being resettled somewhere else. He was such a creature of habit with everything he did that the kids had christened him Robby Robot. I knew he would hate having a new address, having to get used to a different way to go to work, and all the myriad of things that go with change. I also knew full well that I would have to live on my own resources for quite a long time, at least until the house was sold, which I didn't see as happening in the near future. I wanted to be responsible for my own life and decide the direction I would take, and I was prepared to work hard to make it happen.

There Is No "Us" in Retirement

Our marriage really started staggering towards the finish line in 2002, when I began questioning our retirement plans. It concerned me that our marriage had become like train tracks, as it seemed we were travelling in basically the same direction, but was our "destination" really the same? I could have stayed. I could have kept driving him home from the club, golf, or army weekends when he was too drunk to drive. I could have kept hearing the same jokes that I had heard for the past thirty years—half of my life. I could have lived in relative financial security in a house I had worked to help pay for and renovated. But I simply couldn't do it.

As I continued to question Jim about what we would do in retirement, it became clear that there was no "us" in his agenda. His answers were based mainly on how often he would like to play golf each week, and he still intended to play snooker one night a week. I could see years in front of me, collecting him from clubs and driving him home because he was over the alcohol limit. It dawned on me that I didn't figure in his plans. It was all about how he wanted to lead his post-retirement phase, that mental picture didn't thrill me.

As we had a South American daughter-in-law living in Melbourne, I suggested we learn Spanish because I knew Matthew and Bonita planned to bring up their future children bilingual. Jim informed me that he had learned French at school, and it hadn't done him much good, so why bother with Spanish? I thought that if we travelled overseas, it would be a useful language to have, quite apart from the fact that we may go and visit the South American side of the family. Jim did not agree, so that was the end of that suggestion.

Travelling when retired is what a lot of people do these days, hence the term "grey nomads". We could quite easily travel around Australia because we were fit and healthy, and there were always new places to discover. His reply was, "I have seen enough of Australia while I have been in the army, so I don't need to see any more." Okay, thumbs down to suggestion number two.

I was not a person who gave up easily, so I thought I would mention cruising. I knew the army didn't do that! It would not require him to do too much, the bars are always open, there were poker machines on most ships or other forms of gambling, and I thought it would be a good way for me to have a holiday. No meals to prepare, no beds to make, and I wouldn't need to drive anywhere. I thought it would be the perfect holiday.

The response from Jim was, "I get seasick." By this time Jim and I had been together for about twenty-five years, and the only time I had known him to go on anything bigger than a runabout was a navy ship that went outside Sydney Harbour—and yes, he had been sick. But could that possibly have been because at 7.00 a.m. they were already into the beer?

I pointed out that cruise ships these days were very well equipped, comfortable, and air-conditioned, and they provided an inexpensive holiday, relatively speaking. Not to be easily thwarted, I went up to the local travel agent and brought home some brochures; I found a five-day cruise to Melbourne. After dinner I showed it to him and said as it would only be for five days; if he didn't enjoy it, then we need not go on another one, but I would like him to try it. He reluctantly agreed and assured me he would go. "Strike while the iron is hot" was one of my mottoes, so I went to the travel agent the next day and paid the full fare for the cruise, because it was departing in four weeks.

Ten days before the ship was due to sail, Jim announced that he didn't want to go. He said it would be boring and would cost him a week's pay. I got really irritated with him and said, "Why didn't you tell me that in the first place? I am going to forfeit the $1,600 I paid for the fare now." I rang a friend and told her what had happened. She was single with no ties and suggested that she would take Jim's place so that I wouldn't lose the fare I had paid. That suited me because I could still go on the cruise, and he could go to work. I told Jim I had found a friend to travel with me, and he became angry that I was still going.

The ship was late leaving because of some technical difficulty, and we didn't go under the Sydney Harbour Bridge until just on midnight. I lay on a lounge up on the deck and watched all the lights as we pulled away from Sydney. It was a magical way to leave the harbour, but we were then late arriving in Melbourne. A shopping trip to the factory outlets in Richmond had been organised, and I gave the credit card quite a workout. *Serves him right!*

Because Jim hadn't received the idea of travel with any great enthusiasm, I thought ballroom dancing would be something we could do together, because we had met at a social. This idea was also received with the usual lack of enthusiasm and the added rider, "Don't you think I am tired when I come home from work?" I pointed out I was talking about when he was no longer working, but he wouldn't change his mind.

I was persistent, because at that stage I hadn't fully realised that his idea of retirement was quite different from mine. I was desperately trying to find something that we could do together and enjoy as a couple. After all, we were going to have an extra forty working hours per week to be in one house, and I didn't look forward to that with any eagerness.

Little did I know that cruising and dancing would be two of the things Jim did after we split up. I felt really angry with that, but then I reasoned maybe it wasn't the actual activities, but the wife he had to go with, that was the problem. It didn't take him long to find a new girlfriend at a dance, and when he went on a cruise with her, I hoped he would not enjoy it.

Most weeks on Saturday or Sunday at 6.00 a.m., Jim got ready to go to golf—and not quietly, because that was not his way. His idea was, "I am up, so everyone should be up." I was not impressed by this early morning start to a weekend day. For more than two decades I was woken up on golf mornings, because Jim liked company while getting ready for his day out. "Darl, do I have a shirt?" would be his inquiry. Did I care if he had a shirt? Hell no, just leave and let me go back to sleep.

As 2002 moved along to 2003, my running-away account was slowly increasing, and my interest in continuing my marriage was moving in the opposite direction. I was irritable and sarcastic most of the time, and the house was a mess. I couldn't be bothered doing housework and had no pride in the home at all. I was drinking too much, and my head often ached after a night of wine.

Jim mentioned on several occasions that I only worked part-time, and to me, this inferred he thought that I wasn't pulling my weight. To prove this inaccuracy, for two weeks I didn't cook, clean, wash, or iron. He finally noticed that the place looked a bit shabby and the garbage bin was full of takeaway cartons. I pointed out to him that this was what happened when I didn't do what he thought I didn't do.

One night towards the end of 2003, as I held a wine in my hand while I sat on the lounge reading a book, I glanced every now and then at Jim, who was sleeping through the last few minutes of the televised NRL Match of the Day that he just had to watch. There was never negotiation on that subject—football was all he watched, not that he ever went to a game. He was more an armchair expert and liked to have his beer while his team played; he didn't like to have to elbow his way to the bar at the football ground because he might miss an important part of the play. And going to sleep was not missing any of the game?

I learned that as soon as I turned the TV over to another channel, he would snap awake and demand to know the score, as if I had been paying keen attention to the game. After more than two decades of marriage, he still hadn't figured out that I didn't really give a damn what the score was.

Throughout 2004, as with every year that I had known Jim, the playing dates for the two Golf Clubs to which he belonged were written on the calendar as soon as he received the wallet-sized, folded schedules. Those dates then assumed the importance, in his mind, of being carved in stone. No matter whether there were birthdays, anniversaries, or any other celebrations not yet noted on our brand-new calendar still showing January, the golf days took precedence, and all forthcoming social engagements would be accepted or rejected based on their proximity to the golf day.

There was, however, a formula that had to be adhered to, according to Jim. If golf was scheduled for Saturday morning more than ten kilometres from home and during the NRL football season, then Friday night was not to be used for a social outing. The reason for this was that football was often on TV late into the evening, and a lot of beer would be drunk while he sat on the floor, alternating between dozing and jumping up during the ad breaks to go to the fridge for a refill of his beer jug.

It was irrelevant whether I wanted to go out or not, but that was solved when I went by myself; otherwise I stayed home all weekend. My friends commented on several occasions how annoying it was that proposed outings were dependant on the next date of the golfing calendar. It was simply the patchwork of our life.

A patchwork quilt is constructed of perfectly good material, cut up and sewn back together with loving care. Carefully maintained, the quilt will last many years in beautiful condition and give joy to many. If the fabric is neglected, then the resulting deterioration is a barometer of the marriage that the quilt is meant to represent, and it will eventually fall apart from lack of care. And so the quilt of our marriage fell to pieces.

In 2004 we were both turning sixty within three months of each other. I was feeling miserable, so I decided we would have a party in October to celebrate our combined birthdays. Of course the NRL Grand Final fell on the weekend exactly halfway between our birthdays, so we had to move the date of our party. Fortunately we could hire a cruiser for that day that would accommodate the fifty people we planned to invite. I organised a bus to take us from our home to the wharf, and we only had a fifteen-minute window of opportunity to load the boat, because it was a public wharf. The food, decorations, and music were organised by the boat owners; all we had to do on the day was be on time and bring our own cake, soft drinks, and alcohol.

Most of the guests came to our house so that we could go on the bus, because parking was very limited near the wharf. Jim only had to do one thing, and that was to make sure the drinks were put on the bus. The fridge down in the garage was filled with wine and soft drinks, and his homebrew was iced down in Eskys. The guests got on board the bus in front of our place, and the bus then went around to the garage in the back lane for the drinks to be loaded. Well, two out of three ain't bad, as the song goes. When we were about a third of the way to the wharf, I realised that the only drinks that were on board were the beers. The wine and soft drink were still in the garage fridge.

I went absolutely ballistic because I had just about had enough of Jim by October, and he couldn't do this one thing right. His son said for me to get off his back, and I told him he didn't live with him and to mind his own business. I was so angry with Jim that I could hardly speak to him through the party, but I put on a good face because I didn't want to spoil everyone's afternoon; it was supposed to be a celebration. That was the last time I saw most of the people we invited that day.

I did not just throw a tantrum one day and walk out, even though Jim swore he had no idea what was coming. I thought that when I moved out of the bedroom two years previously and hardly spoke to him each night (mainly because he watched the news at 5.30, 6.00, and 7.00, and then was consumed by what was on the TV), he would get the message that I wasn't happy, but he obviously didn't notice or didn't care.

On 9 December 2004 our fridge broke down. As most people would realise, there was a fair bit of food to be refrigerated at that time of the year. Not wanting to leave it too long before we replaced the fridge, I rang a refrigeration mechanic and gave him the symptoms over the phone. He said it sounded as though it needed replacing, because it would cost more than it was worth to repair it. We had had the fridge for a number of years, and with the kitchen renovation it was a very neat fit, so there would not be a lot of choice given the size of the cavity into which it had to fit. I measured the fridge and the available space around it, taking into account the distance it had to be from the back wall for ventilation and the plug. I am an organised person and would not dream of going to buy a refrigerator to fit in a limited space without measuring it first.

Friday was my day off, and I went to Bing Lee at Westfield. While there I phoned Jim to tell him that there were only two fridges that would fit in that space. One had the freezer on the top, which was like our current model, and the other had the refrigerator on the top. They were similar in price, so I asked him if he had any preference. Jim was such a creature of habit and chose the one with the same configuration as the fridge that had just died.

However, while I was still in the shop and organising delivery, thinking of the various borrowed Esky's down in the garage where I was trying to keep things cool, he phoned me to say not to buy anything, because he wanted me to go to a few other places and compare prices to see if there were any other alternatives. It was already late in the afternoon, I had found only two models out of a very good range, and we could have it delivered tomorrow, so I told him I wasn't going to waste time looking around for something that may not exist. He said he would go looking the next morning. This amazed me because he has never wanted to be involved in buying any household goods, but perhaps the icy atmosphere in the house had struck some nerve.

Saturday morning, while I was still in bed because it was only 8.00 a.m., Jim set out to find a new fridge. I suggested a few places he could go, but no, Jim went straight up to the store I had been the previous day, where they showed him the same two fridges, quoted the same prices, and said that if we had bought a fridge yesterday, we could have had it delivered that morning. He rang me and couldn't understand why I exploded when he commented that the fridge could have been delivered Saturday if "we" had bought it yesterday. I could have strangled him, except he was two kilometres away, which was probably lucky for him.

The next day I went up to my daughter's place because she was down at Bonneville Bay on the south coast of NSW having some furniture delivered to their holiday home, and John needed to go down there and help. Their return to Sydney was uncertain, so Karen asked me if I could mind Cameron and Jade for the rest of Sunday and until her return on Monday, which was also when our new fridge was to be delivered. I asked Jim to make sure that he emptied the fridge out, because I wouldn't be home that night, and it had to be ready to be taken away the next afternoon.

The store had promised they would phone between 1.00 and 4.00 p.m. to give an approximate time of delivery so that I could be there. The rain was torrential, and I could hardly see through the windscreen, but luckily I could put the kids in the car while in Karen's garage to keep them dry, because she hadn't yet arrived home.

When I got back to my place, the old fridge was in the middle of the kitchen floor, supposedly ready to be taken to the tip or wherever dead fridges went. There was thunder and hail by this time, and the driver wanted to get the old fridge out and the new one in before the weather got any worse. When they moved the old fridge, one of the deliverymen mentioned that there were two gouges in the kitchen vinyl floor, but they assured me that they had not done the damage. I didn't even look at the new fridge as the deliverymen plugged it in, and I had to get Cameron and Jade home to their place. When I got home and Jim arrived from work, I pointed out the damage to the floor. He said he had ripped it because he hadn't put something under the fridge before pulling it out into the centre of the kitchen. I was not impressed because I had suggested just that manoeuvre the day before, to prevent damage to the vinyl. It had only been replaced three months before, when Jim took it into his head to make hot lead sinkers one afternoon and put them on a cloth on the floor, which then burned right through into the vinyl.

It was then that I realised the front of the fridge didn't have any of my usual magnets, particularly Cameron's first Christmas photo, which was in a magnetic frame. When I asked Jim where the magnets and photo were, he looked perplexed for a moment and then said, "I didn't know you wanted me to take them off, so I guess they have gone to the tip." My language was rather colourful, to say the least, running along the lines of what sort of an idiot was I married to. His excuse was that I hadn't told him to take them off the fridge, so it wasn't actually his fault.

But when he realised that his favourite beer jug for his home brew and six of his glasses were also on their way to the tip, he wasn't as blasé as he had been about what mattered to me. I was furious with him, upset that Cameron's photo was gone, and fed up with his excuse that I hadn't told him to take them off the front of the fridge.

That Tuesday night, when I started to prepare dinner, I realised that some of the vegetables were missing, and I asked him where they were. He said he had put them in the old beer fridge in the garage (which wasn't plugged in), and he didn't think they were any good now. God, give me strength! I can see how some women are driven to commit a homicidal end to a marital relationship.

On 15 December 2004, Jim and I went up to Pennington RSL for our weekly cheap meal, which was really a misnomer because it cost me about sixty dollars for two bistro meals, two wines for me, and several beers for Jim, plus whatever change made its way down the throats of the ever waiting poker machines situated between the bar and our table. Usually we sat with some other people who were Western football fans, and the previous game would be dissected and reinvented before moving on to talk of the game coming up this week. I was bored to tears. I was not, never had been, and never would be a football fanatic.

By the end of that night I was not in any mood to be polite anymore, and given that the group ignored me for most of the time we shared their table, I decided I would take a book; at least I would be enjoying myself until it was time to get the courtesy bus home. Because of the state of the homeward-bound club members, I had christened it the Silly Bus.

Sunday 19 December was the Gala Golf Day. I had told Jim I wasn't sitting around in the heat waiting for him to be ready to come home; he could either make a time to be collected, or ring me when he was ready to leave the club. The year before he rang me when he was supposedly ready to leave, and then he went in to have another beer and couldn't understand why I was cranky about having to wait in the car in the midday heat. I had had shorts and a top on that wouldn't pass the dress code, and that was the only reason I didn't go in and drag him out of the club. I'd waited a half hour, which was more than he deserved, and then left to go home.

His brother brought him home, and Jim was reasonably sober for a change because he had only drunk light beer. My greeting was certainly less than enthusiastic because I had done a lot of thinking through the week and realised that I was desperately unhappy. It was probably bad timing to have a full, in-depth, and meaningful conversation with Jim after a golf day, but it was now or never as far as I was concerned. I told him that he took no responsibility for himself or anything else. He didn't want to go anywhere with me and always said, "We can't afford it," but he could afford golf weekends away and whatever else suited him. No expense was spared when we went interstate to see his son and daughter-in-law, or our friends in Queensland. I was sick to death of hearing the same things over and over, like a broken record. I was tired of him sitting on the other side of the lounge room every evening and watching the same programs night after night. Football was on the television all weekend, even when he wasn't actually in the house, but I couldn't have the radio on in case he heard the score; apparently that would spoil his pleasure in watching the game later on in the day.

For a lot of years in the early part of our marriage, he used to help me a bit in the house: do the fruit and vegetable shopping on the weekend, wash my car and maintain it, and bathe the dogs. Over the last few years he had decided he didn't feel like doing any of these chores, so they transferred from his list to mine because he couldn't be bothered with it. No negotiation, just transferred! Great for him, but as he was fond of saying to me, "You only work part-time." If ever there was a phrase that would put my hackles up, it was that one; it made me feel that I wasn't pulling my weight, and he had no regard for the effort I actually put into the household, although as far as effort and marriage went, that was diminishing rapidly.

When I went out with friends to the Opera House, Ensemble Theatre, or anywhere for that matter, he was like a little lost child worrying about whether there was something for him to eat. He was well over twenty-one and could quite easily get something to eat, because there was plenty of food in the cupboards, fridge, and freezer. It was this hopeless, "look after me" attitude that drove more than one nail into the marital coffin. I tried to explain to him that I was not his mother, and had I wanted another child, I would have given birth to one, not married one. It became painfully obvious to me that if I was going to be alone while he went to golf, snooker, and whatever else he had decided his retirement consisted of, then I might as well be by myself. At least then I could do and be whatever I wanted. I gave little thought as to what the rest of my life was going to be like, but I was confident I would be okay. I could work, I was in good health, and I could make another life for myself.

On 20 December 2004 I decided I had had enough. Enough of the isolation of being alone in a marriage; enough of the life I was leading that didn't have much of me in it. I packed a bag and walked out of a twenty-six-year marriage with no fear that I would not survive. I was tired of being half of a couple, but not half of a partnership. We had no interests in common, and when retirement was discussed, it was only ever about what he was going to do, with no consideration of what I might want from the later years of our life.

My husband met me in the doorway and said, "So, is this final?" I replied, "It sure is. I've had enough." My stepson and his wife were coming from Melbourne for the funeral of a friend, and they were arriving at about 8.00 p.m. I hoped they had had something to eat on the plane, because there was no hot meal waiting at my place.

I had asked my daughter in a phone call that afternoon if I could stay at her place for a few weeks while they were on holiday, so that I had somewhere to go. I was out of there. It wasn't that I hadn't warned him I was unhappy. It was simply that he chose not to listen.

Relationship Post-Mortem

I didn't realise that the death of a marriage also meant the end of many dreams, both shared and singular. We had been together for half of our sixty years on this earth, and we had shared the upbringing of two children: Matthew, his son from his first marriage, and Karen, my daughter from my first marriage. Fortunately we had no children from our marriage, so a third child did not need to take sides.

Friends also felt as though they needed to divide into different camps, and the separated couple had no control over which friends took whose side. Family also fell by the wayside because they felt they could no longer be there for both partners.

And so the circle of friends and family first reacted with shock that this particular couple they knew so well was in fact not as happy as believed to be. It became a source of fear for some people that this marital discontent they have witnessed might in some way be contagious, and that it would upset their own happy lives.

Then there were the questions. A post mortem was conducted by all and sundry on the marriage that everyone thought had the hallmarks of longevity. To the outside world, we were a normal couple. We had a house (albeit mortgaged), children, and pets. We were of a similar age and background and had been together for thirty years. We went on holidays together, had friends and relatives to our home for dinner parties, hosted barbeques, and had quite good relationships with our ex-partners.

Some people accepted the reasons given, but others wanted to dissect the marital corpse down to the skeleton, as though knowing what went wrong would give them a yardstick by which to measure their relationship against the "failed" one of their friends, and they hoped they got their calculations correct. Perhaps they thought this knowledge would protect their marriage or relationship, but sadly it would not.

Nobody knows what goes on behind closed doors (I think they wrote a song with that line in it) because people do not generally air their grievances in public until the relationship has deteriorated to such a degree that it is not worth saving. Fear is part of couples taking stock of their situation, and they come out of this comparison feeling a little more secure (even bordering on smug), or scared that they have uncovered flaws or cracks of which they were previously unaware. *Could the same thing happen to us?* they wonder. Yes, it most certainly could.

The quantity of years in a marriage is by no means a guide to the quality; unlike good wine or first-edition books, it does not necessarily get better and more valuable with age. Couples can become like the two hands of one person, where each knows what the other is thinking—or like us, they can become as far apart as train tracks, where they travel side by side as a couple but never emotionally meet up.

Not arguing in front of other people or having an angry shouting match in a public place is also not a barometer of the atmosphere in a marriage. Sometimes people quietly seethe for a long time and are "yes dear" and "no dear" in public, but in private they hardly have a civil conversation because they are then devoid of an audience to observe their misery.

A blazing row is often a cause for alarm by anyone witnessing it, but like a tropical storm, it is all noise and wind, and it's over in a short time and followed by sunshine and clear waters. There are those couples that enjoy being together whether in a palace or a tent, and they will talk, laugh, love, and live life to the fullest no matter what the circumstances. They will be secretly envied by most people who come in contact with them—but again, their private life is just that, private.

Wealth is not an automatic guarantee of a healthy marriage, either, and it can even contribute to why a couple drifts apart. Due to the pressure of outside obligations to maintain and build this wealth, not just for the couple concerned but to perhaps start a dynasty for generations to come, the relationship can fail. With this wealth accumulation can come long work hours, excessive travel, and missing family occasions and time with the family to just be a family and enjoy each other's company in a simple, sustainable lifestyle.

If the wealth fails to keep the family together, then the knives come out in the form of lawyers, real estate agents, financial advisers, and others who have an incredible talent for smelling blood and the rotting carcass of a marriage that appeared to have all the right ingredients to succeed. But fail it does, and there are the spoils to be divided up with the appropriate fees to be paid, while a life is picked apart and letters are written to the "other side" about who gets the cake tins.

In 2004, we became one of those couples.

The Single Life—Again

Being single again did not daunt me as much as it did Jim. He was very concerned about how he was going to live on a lot less money but with similar expenses to what we had before I left, although he had a better income than I did. My response was, "Welcome to my world." I knew that it would be difficult, but I was prepared for that because I was more aware of our financial situation than Jim ever was. He had never really taken much interest in this part of our life. I knew that I had to set up a new household but had no fear that I wouldn't cope—somehow.

About a week after I left, Jim phoned me at my daughter's place to ask if I was *really* cranky with him, because I had taken his Cold Power and Napi-San. I explained to him that I had left the liquid detergent for him, and I didn't even know he used Napi-San because he had never washed anything before. I got off the phone and laughed out loud. How bizarre that after all the years we had been together, he was more concerned about me taking "his" washing powder than the fact that our marriage was over.

Jim questioned me in a rather irritable tone of voice during another phone call about what I was buying for the flat I was moving into at Mum's, and why I was spending the money. He was the primary buyer on the credit card, and he was obviously concerned that I was spending "his" money. I reassured him that I would reimburse him for whatever I spent. I couldn't get a credit card because I didn't have any history, being the second purchaser on his card.

It took months to remove my name from credit cards, car registration, insurance, telephone accounts, medical funds, Medicare card, and all the other assorted household minutiae that went along with a marriage. Any bonus points accrued went to him and not me, because he was the primary cardholder—rather unfair, I thought, but those were the rules. Jim wasn't interested in attending to this, so again it was left up to me; he kept reminding me that I was the one who had left, so it was my problem.

I knew he was deeply hurt that I had ended our marriage, but he didn't seem to be able to come to grips with the idea that he was now on his own. He had to decide what to eat, what to buy, and how to cook it; he had to learn to pay bills over the phone etc. I had a phone call one weekend asking me if I would go up and help him with phone banking, as he didn't know how to do it. Of course he didn't know because he had never wanted to learn and now had come the time when he had no choice.

While I was there, he asked me to write out some simple recipes so he could cook up enough food on the weekend to feed himself all week. He had previously rejected the idea of me cooking food and then freezing it, but somehow he had gotten over this aversion in order to survive.

He hadn't quite come to grips with the fact that I wasn't coming back into the marriage, and he asked me if he could take me out to dinner at a Chinese restaurant. He appeared at the door with a potted plant in one hand and a bottle of wine in the other. He told me he wasn't going to drink beer and would have a soft drink so that he could drive me home. All those years we were married, and this was one of about six occasions when he was the one who drove the return trip. It was so frustrating because this was one thing that had been an issue between us. He previously drove to our destination and drank while we were there, and then I drove home. It wasn't fair and really made me angry—and here we were separated, and he offered to drive. Go figure.

Over dinner we spoke about our present situation, and again I told him I wasn't coming back to the marriage. The usual subjects came up, as I knew they would because he was so predictable. It was as though he is a vinyl record with the needle stuck in a track and on continuous play. I knew he didn't like the amount of time I spent with my friends, but at least I got to go somewhere. I pointed out that if he didn't want to go out with me, why should I stay home? I explained that it was not expensive entertainment I was looking for, but something simple like going to a park, buying a coffee, and sitting in the sun while reading the paper or feeding the ducks. None of these ideas seemed to interest him.

He told me that I was the hardest person he had ever met, and that I have not the least bit of softness in me. That hurt a bit because he had never expressed that opinion before, and I wasn't sure if he was just having a go at me because I left, or if it was something that he had been seething about for a while. I asked him why he would want me back if I was so hard and kept him at arm's length emotionally. He had no answer for that.

We discussed our money issues, and I agreed to pay half the health fund, my own car insurance, my mobile phone account, the Internet, and my own telephone bill—in total about two hundred dollars per month. I arranged a direct debit from my account to his so that there could not be a future dispute about whether or not I had kept my part of the bargain. As the dinner came to an end it was obvious—to me, at least—that nothing had been resolved and that this marriage had reached its "use by" date.

I had left my dog Zoe with Jim until I got settled at Beresford, and he suggested that we take her for a walk one Sunday afternoon. It was really weird to go on outings with him that we hadn't done while we were married, even though I had asked on many occasions. While we were out walking, he commented that my daughter and son-in-law didn't have great communication, and I was struck dumb by this observation. He didn't see that this was one of the main reasons our marriage had failed. Maybe he couldn't see the forest for the trees? Whenever I had tried in the past to discuss controversial issues with Jim, or to get some sort of a decision out of him, he would walk away while I was still talking to him. With a lack of input from him, I then would decide for myself what needed to be done, but he was quite happy to criticise my decision. I thought, *If you don't want to participate, how can you object to the outcome?* It was a no-win situation that greatly contributed to the breakdown in our relationship.

Looking back on our marriage, it was a wonder that it lasted as long as it did. There were so many differences in our attitude towards money, family, and lifestyle, and very few similarities. The saying goes that opposites attract, and that may well be so, but can they live in harmony? I doubted it after this experience.

A few weeks into our separation, Jim arrived at my daughter's place on Saturday morning to play with the grandkids, and I happened to be there. He talked about how lonely he was, and I again reminded him that it is possible to be alone but not lonely, as I was now, whereas when I was married to him, I was lonely but not alone. He didn't seem to grasp the difference.

He told me that my leaving him had been the biggest kick in the backside he had ever had. He wanted someone to blame—other than himself, of course—so he chose a friend of mine with whom I had gone to the Opera House and the Ensemble Theatre on a regular basis because we had season tickets. I told him that she had had nothing to do with me leaving him, but he vehemently disputed this. Didn't he think I had a brain and could work things out for myself?

We had another phone conversation one evening, when he rang me about cooking tuna Mornay and whether it could be frozen. As usual he asked the question and disagreed with the answer. I told him to do whatever he liked with his bloody dinner. He then asked me if I took a bag of frozen vegetables from the freezer that he had stapled shut. For goodness sake!

He also complained that I spoke sharply to him when he didn't listen to what was happening and when he does stupid things, like the fridge episode. I just got frustrated with him, especially when he pretended to know something and told it like gospel, when it is a complete fabrication. I was told that I intimidated him, but he missed having someone to talk to. Well, for years I had been right there, just across the lounge room, if he wanted someone to have a conversation with, but somehow the television took precedence. I hoped he and the TV were very happy together in their new life.

As the weeks became months, I settled into my new life, but Jim still struggled with his single status. He was still hopeful that I would return to the marriage, but I constantly told him that it was over and he needed to move on, as I had. He started going dancing, which he wouldn't do with me, and met a lady there. He subsequently went on a couple of cruises with the same lady, and I hoped for a typhoon.

Jim was upset that I had already made an irrevocable decision to not return to the marriage. He told me it was too soon to make such a decision about throwing away thirty years, but I told him it was more about throwing away the next twenty-five years, and I was not prepared to do that. I wanted the last third of my life to be more fulfilling, and if I had to do that by myself, then so be it.

Add into the mix a stepson who thought he knew all the answers to his father's marriage problems, and it became as volatile as nitro-glycerine. I met Jim when Matthew was less than two years old, and Matthew had spent a great deal of the intervening years with us on weekends and holidays. He took it upon himself to interrogate me about what had happened with our marriage and why it was now at an end. I told Matthew a few home truths about his father, some of which he already knew because I had written him a letter a year ago, and some he did not. Matthew sensed my frustration and told me he would try to explain my feelings to Jim, but this made me rather angry, because obviously he would take his father's side in anything that was said.

Matthew questioned me about whether I still loved Jim, and I said, "No, and I don't respect him, either." I explained to Matthew that Jim would prefer to stay home and sit in the lounge room watching television, going to golf, and playing snooker, rather than going out on any social occasion with me. However, if I did manage to get him to go anywhere, I ran the risk of being embarrassed by his drinking and bad language once he had sufficient alcohol on board. At the end of the night, it would be me driving him home again, and I was over the whole scenario.

I was basically tired of the same old thing year in and year out, and I had no hope that anything would change. I knew in my heart of hearts that even the fact that I had walked out on the marriage would not be enough to fix the cracks that had widened to crevasses, especially over the last few years. I knew Jim would try to appear that he had changed for a while, but habit would overcome his good intentions, and we would be back to square one.

My daughter also had her say, and she seemed to take Jim's side against me. Karen said that if I was not going back to Jim, I should tell him now and put the house on the market. I explained that Jim wanted me to wait six months before making a final decision. Karen was of the opinion that Jim would keep trying to change, and then in six months I would tell him I am not coming back. I tried to explain to her that as far as I was concerned the marriage was over, but Jim was not able to accept that at this moment.

I hated being put on the spot about things that were really nothing to do with anyone else; where I lived and what I did with my share of the assets was really nobody else's business.

Karen asked me if I was going to mind Cameron and Jade on Tuesday and Wednesday while she did some coaching, and I was very short with her. She wanted to know what was wrong, and I kept answering, "Nothing", because I really didn't want to discuss it anymore. I had had enough for one day. She phoned me when I got home, again to see what was wrong, so I told her in no uncertain terms that I didn't think she had been supportive when I was moving from my long-time home to the granny flat. Her explanation to that was, "How could I, when I have two children?" Karen was of the impression that because I had a lot of single and divorced friends, they had encouraged me to leave. The flat being empty and my running-away account being full was all I needed to make a break for a new life.

I tried to put forward my side of the story, which was that I no longer wanted to be in a partnership that felt like I was married to myself. I had raised my daughter, was holding down a part-time job, and was helping her with minding her children. Outside of that, I also wanted to be able to go to the theatre and movies, and have holidays at places that interested me, but Jim didn't want to be part of that journey. He had had the choice but preferred to have his own life, and he wasn't prepared to expand his horizons one bit.

It hurt me when she said that I was hard and rarely cried. Neither did she, for that matter, but she mentioned Christmas morning when she was upset by Jim's teary phone call, and it hadn't seemed to move me one bit. She obviously didn't understand that my marriage had been moving towards its eventual end for a few years, and my emotions were all worn out where Jim was concerned.

It was time to move on and have a new life, on my own terms.

Haven or Hell—The Granny Flat

The flat, my new residence starting in January 2005, had been built back in the early 1950s as a workshop on the bottom level and a garage on the top. My father had used the workshop to make many Christmas and birthday presents for my brother and me. It originally had a dirt floor, which didn't matter when it housed hand tools (before power was put from the house to the flat), but when my friends wanted somewhere to live back in 1966, Dad said he would turn it into a place for them if they helped convert it. The deal was done, and my friends lived there for a few years before they bought their first home.

Many newly married couples followed, and some added to the décor and some detracted. By the time I got there, it was a mismatch of ideas and materials. I didn't have any furniture, and my mother had loaned me a single bed, which was the only size that would fit in the narrow bedroom. There was already a built-in wardrobe of sorts, but I needed a chest of drawers, a bedside table, a lamp, and a new ceiling light.

The flat had become empty in October 2004 because my friend Fay, who had lived there for fourteen years, suffered cardiac arrest while in hospital, and it was decided that she could no longer live in a two-storey building with a steep, spiral staircase. Because of her ongoing heart condition, it was decided that she needed to be with someone, and she moved in with her son. When I realised that there was a vacant place I could live in, it was like a chink of light showing at the edge of a very dark door.

In December 2004, when I realised that I could not live with Jim much longer, I felt that if I could move into the flat, I would be able to survive financially. Mum was widowed and lonely, and I thought that it would be mutually beneficial. After Dad died, Mum had asked me nearly every week to do something for her, sometimes as simple as replacing a light globe, changing the batteries in a remote control, or getting the garage door open. I also set her hair every Saturday. Now I wouldn't have to drive eight kilometres to do so.

The warning bells should have rung loud and clear in my head when Mum made it quite plain that if I got tangled up with another male, I would have to leave. At that stage I didn't want another complication in my life, so I wasn't unduly worried, though I should have been. I knew she viewed every male with suspicion, even her own son and grandson.

For me, it would mean having somewhere I could get myself back together and decide what to do with the rest of my life. I had been married for more than half my years on earth and had never lived by myself. This was to be my first time, and it was exciting and scary all at once. I wanted the flat to be my home, but it was nothing compared to the house I was leaving behind. The floor plan was difficult and the colour was not to my taste, but it was a haven for me at that time.

One of the first places I went when I moved to the flat in January 2005 was to Bunnings. I knew I would need paint, brushes, tools, kitchen appliances, and some garden tools. Mum had a big yard, and I offered to look after the gardens and her car, because she wouldn't take any rent from me.

I bought a flat-pack dining setting, which had to come down steep and uneven stone outdoor steps, and through the narrow window, to be put in the dining room on the bottom floor. I then arranged, over the next few weeks, to have a small lounge made with one chair, because the living area was very small and the door into the top floor was too narrow to fit a standard size. With thick sandstone walls as a base, it was cool all year round, though sometimes a bit too cold in the winter. Conversely, the top floor had large picture windows with a wonderful view over the golf course, but it was extremely hot in the summer, having no insulation in the roof. A metal spiral staircase linking the two floors was located in the right-hand back corner and required very careful negotiation. The stair treads were metal, wedge-shaped, and very narrow. Carrying groceries to the kitchen downstairs meant making sure I had a hand free to hold onto the rail. After one of my shopping trips, I got a bag of groceries caught between the uprights on the handrail, and I was almost pitched headfirst down the rest of the stairs.

The kitchen, eating area, and a bathroom measuring 1.5 metres by 2 metres (smaller than most en suites) were on the ground floor, but the toilet was located across the yard and directly under the dining room of my mother's house. This location had a distinct disadvantage on wet and rainy nights, but it certainly improved my bladder control because the thought of getting cold and wet lacked appeal.

On the top floor was a very narrow bedroom of two metres by six metres, with one window that unfortunately faced the hot westerly afternoon sun, and a built-in wardrobe that had no doors or drawers. The carpet was an old one of mine that had been on the floor for fourteen years, so it really had to go. It was extremely ugly and very worn, and I couldn't live with it long term.

I knew that I had enough money in my running-away account to replace the carpet and repaint the awful mint and caramel walls and trim. Green had never been a favourite colour of mine for decorating, and I decided that in such a small space, beige was the way to go. Due to the inconsistencies in height of the walls, skirting, windows, ceiling, and doors, all one colour was the best option. I recruited a friend who came with me to a carpet company, and I bought an off-cut, the cheapest way to go, and arranged for it to be laid the next day. I couldn't move any furniture in until the carpet was down, and then I had to think about what I could actually fit in the space of a flat that was four metres wide and six metres long on the top floor, and one metre smaller on the bottom because of the thickness of the stone walls and the 1.5-metre square stairwell.

It was what the real estate agents would describe as compact. There was also a really ugly, faux brick dividing wall across half of the living area with some sort of tacky vinyl-clad chipboard unit built by a former tenant. Louvre bar doors divided the living area from the bedroom and were the final touch in a rather ugly décor. The bar doors were painted a chocolate brown, which certainly didn't make the room look any larger.

I hadn't taken any furniture from our home and only returned in the first week of January to pack some towels, sheets, china and cutlery, and some art that I had done; the rest was personal possessions. There really wasn't any point taking furniture or appliances that I had no room to store. The flat was so small that very little would fit through the only entry door, and I felt that a fresh start would be better. I didn't want to take things from Jim just because I could.

Two friends and my mother came to help, and we used two cars for half a day to transport everything the eight kilometres from my lovely home to my new home of a granny flat. Quite a comedown in size and quality, but it was where I had to be at that stage of my life. Unpacking didn't take long, and then I had to decide how I was going to live in this very small and unattractive place.

There was an area under my mother's kitchen that was not quite high enough to stand upright in, but it was somewhere I could store the things I couldn't fit in the flat and, later on, the garden tools I bought. The area hadn't been touched since Dad got sick many years before and was full of old paint tins, excess tiles from both of the holiday houses he had built, lengths of timber, and a box trailer axle. Goodness only knows how he managed to get that in there. It took weeks to clean out, but it was worth having the extra storage space. It was rather damp and had a dirt floor, but I got some cheap vinyl flooring and put it down on the ground. It formed an effective barrier against the damp, and with some second-hand metal racking, I managed to fill it up with what I couldn't fit in the flat or didn't need straight away.

Added to this less than ideal residence was the proximity to the untamed greenery that had crept up from the golf course, behind the flat at the outer edge of the property, and almost taken over all the spare space down the side of the flat. It was such a lush environment because there was a sixty-centimetre storm water pipe that emptied all the rainwater from the street down the side of the building. On a wet day it sounded like I was living beside a waterfall, and the water continued long after the rain had stopped.

At night I could hear frogs, and in the morning birds woke me with their many calls, but the weekend golfers also managed to add to the cacophony at dawn. I had some other unwanted creatures such as cockroaches that seemed to find their way in through crevices I couldn't even see, and ants that had decided this was to be their home. No amount of spraying or stamping on the ants managed to stop the constant parade through the door and windows.

I had decided to leave my miniature fox terrier, Zoe, at home with Jim until I got myself settled and made sure she couldn't escape from the property where I had moved. However, over the next six years, Zoe managed to get out when there was a thunderstorm or lightning, no matter what barriers I put in her way. She was a very determined little dog, but she was terrified of storms and could jump the most secure fences. It was impossible to keep her in because the bottom level had a very low wall, and she could jump it and disappear down into the golf course. Mum wouldn't let me put anything on top of the wall to stop her getting out, so it was a constant concern if I was at work when a storm was predicted. When I was at home, I would often hear Mum yelling out to Zoe to get off the wall, and her voice sounded like dragging fingernails down a chalkboard. I couldn't guarantee that Zoe would go into the flat and stay there, even though the door was open. She took flight and ran as far as she could, but I managed to get her back each time.

When I had been there about three years, the walkway that allowed access to the doorway into the flat needed replacing. It was very unsteady, mostly due to the amount of water that had been rushing down and through the upright timbers, and it had rotted some of them. I asked my son-in-law if he could organise someone to help fix it. It was so steep that it took many more hours than anticipated, and eventually four thousand dollars later, fortunately at mates' rates, it was safe and finished. I could then go from the backyard to the doorway and into the flat without fear of falling through the rotten timbers. It was much more dangerous than I had originally thought, and I hated to think what would have happened if it had been left much longer to be replaced.

Mum had been so used to Dad doing all the repairs around the place that maintenance had been neglected. The walkway down the side of the flat was just one of the things around the house that had been left to fall into disrepair. In all fairness to Mum, she was not really capable of keeping things up to scratch. For almost fifty years she had never had to consider what was happening outside the house, because Dad had always taken care of the yard. After Dad had a cerebral haemorrhage in 1990, nothing much got done outside except the obvious things, such as lawns and gardens, for which Mum had to pay.

I had made a deal with Mum to look after the gardens, and I started on the fernery in the backyard. It was overgrown with weeds, ivy, and all sorts of plants that had grown there by the seeds being deposited in bird poo. Dad had built the fernery, and it was certainly a sturdy structure because he had always used timber that was far heavier than it needed to be, but mostly it was whatever was available from the side of the road during clean-up weeks.

It was a big job because it hadn't been done for so many years, but I persisted, because this was where I was going to live for however long that I could, and I liked to view nice gardens. However, my mother's idea of nice and mine were poles apart, which was typical of our whole relationship.

Mum liked flowers; I liked native shrubs that could be trimmed every year and would almost look after themselves. Mum preferred plants in pots, and I wanted them in the ground. Compromise became the name of the game, and eventually the fernery was finished almost to her satisfaction. As she pointed out, it was her yard, and she would have it how she wanted it. It took so much time to look after this one piece of garden, because she didn't want any mulch or bark on the top of the ground, even though I explained it would help keep the plant roots moist and the weeds to a minimum.

Then I moved on to tidying up the front yard. That was even worse because I had to work in amongst about twenty rose bushes that hadn't been cut back for years, and they were straggly and tangled into each other. Again we disagreed on what the front yard should look like, and I certainly wasn't winning even though I was buying the plants and new soil. I could see that if all the gardens followed the pretty flower display that Mum wanted, I would spend half my life watering the garden and a large chunk of time replanting when the flowers died off. Oh well, a deal was a deal, but it certainly didn't give me much joy.

The last part of this gardening challenge was to do something with the large area that was outside the bottom level of the flat. Dad had built an oval concrete swimming pool down there when I was about ten years old—quite a talking point back in the 1950s. We backed onto bush, which was pre-golf course, so he had put a drain in the deepest end of the pool with an ordinary bath plug that could be removed to let the water out. There was no such thing as pool filters and pumps then, and even if there had been, there was no electricity in the yard for them to run on. It was a simple matter of emptying out the pool when it was required and filling it up again with a garden hose.

Cooking and Living as One

After spending all my married life shopping and cooking for at least three people, it was very difficult to cut down to purchasing for just a single. It was also uneconomical, because most recipes were for two or four, and packaging was targeted at the same number of people in a household. It was challenging, if not impossible, to find recipes for lone cooks. For the first few weeks that I lived alone, recipes from the Internet did not help because the ones for a single person were few and far between. This must be a huge market for cookbooks, because we don't all live as couples, and statistics prove that single-person households are increasing.

When I started living by myself, for the first time in my life I set the table as I had done for all those years, but for one, and I sat there to eat my meal. That didn't last long because I couldn't see the television to watch the evening news, and I had nobody to talk to, not even a pet at that stage. Out of the packed away boxes I found a tray I had painted when I had done folk art, and that became my portable table. I wondered how many single people actually sat at the table. Did they become sofa suppers like me?

If I bought a large economy pack of cereal, I found myself chewing on it for weeks. Not only did I get tired of the same breakfast every day, but sometimes it was a race to finish the packet before the indwelling weevils woke up from their slumber and flew out with the first flakes of grain to hit my plate. That was very distasteful first thing in the morning, and it was not the way I wanted to get my daily allowance of protein.

I also found that even the smallest tub of tomato paste grew blue mould when it was put back in the fridge with the idea that it would be used in another recipe some other day; generally it went into the bin before that next recipe materialised. There were hints that one could cover the tomato paste in oil to stop the mould, but somehow I never remembered to do that.

I got to the stage where I grilled a piece of meat and had it with the salad I had yesterday, the day before, and the one before that. Three-day-old coleslaw developed a vinegar smell that made it very unappetising, to say the least.

Cooking enough for two and freezing half lost its charm long before the ice crystals started to form on the top and disguised the contents. Again, I could have labelled the containers, but somehow I never actually got around to it. Either I couldn't find a pen, or else the labels wouldn't stick. Opening the freezer cabinet and peering in at several UFOs (unidentified food objects) was enough to send me to the local fish 'n' chips shop, where I could recite the menu without even looking at it.

I had a number of cookbooks with good, nutritious meals on each page, but the number of ingredients read like my weekly shopping list. It was also hard to find small appliances in which to cook. Most of them were "family size", whatever that was. A lonely egg and one piece of bacon looked all wrong in a frying pan that used up half the kitchen bench, and the washing up took longer than the cooking.

Making nutritious meals for one person was something that I gave up on after about six months. It took me longer to cook the meal and clean the kitchen afterwards than the minutes required eating what I had prepared. I even thought at one stage that if I could find a few single people who lived nearby, we could each cook a meal for four, break it down into containers, and swap it amongst ourselves. It was great in theory but not practical, and it was hard to find people who were interested in this idea.

Next I decided that because I lived quite close to the local RSL Club and was a member, I could make use of their brasserie a few nights a week. One of the downsides to this idea was that one could try to make wise choices regarding salt and fat content when cooking at home, but because there was no indication on the menu, it was all guesswork. The price of the meal also came into it and was above what it would cost to buy the ingredients separately and cook it at home, even if one included 50 per cent wastage.

I didn't like to sit at a table and eat by myself while staring across the club while I chewed my meal, so I decided that I would take a book to read. That would have worked okay if I had thought to take a rubber band with me to keep the book open while I cut up my food. I finished up with as much gravy splattered on the book as was left on my plate. The next time I ventured into the club, I was the only female in the restaurant amongst a lot of men, and I felt very conspicuous. Perhaps they didn't even notice me, but I ate my meal with indigestion-forming speed, gulped down my glass of Chardonnay, and left as quickly as my high heels would let me. It was obvious that eating out alone was not how I wanted to consume my meals, either. I felt too awkward walking into a club by myself, sitting at a table for two with the other chair vacant, and managing to keep the gravy off my book.

It was back to the drawing board. I decided that I would try the idea of having my meals for the day home-delivered. This was not an inexpensive option, but I gave it a try. The meals were generally nutritious and the variety was good, but after a few weeks it all started to taste like the cardboard it was packed in, and it was not cheap.

Chinese takeaway, pizza, and hamburgers were possibilities for the single population. However, there would be leftovers because the Asian food containers were not a one-person portion. Whatever I ordered seemed to need rice (either boiled or fried) to accompany it, and therefore I had two containers of food. Most Asian food was not better the next day, and therefore the surplus became leftovers or a meal for the dog—but my dog wasn't keen on it, so the food became another thing in the fridge. Pizza could be gently reheated in the oven the next day for a hungry teenager, but I didn't have one of those and was not one myself.

Each fortnight, on the weekend prior to garbage collection, I cleaned out the fridge. I was appalled, though not surprised, at how much waste one person could accumulate, especially when that person didn't eat at home very often. There were the aforementioned tomato paste tubs, salad leaves that had reached their "use by" date several days before, tomatoes that had gone to mush, and half a zucchini.

It was quite amazing, the types of fur that could grow on vegetables that were deposited in the fridge with clean, shiny outer skins in the last two weeks. Their demise into mushy objects—as zucchini seem to do—grey circles growing on carrots and oranges, and funny little extensions poking out of potatoes was an amazing microcosm quietly sitting in the crisper tray of the refrigerator.

I tried buying fewer vegetables, but whatever vegetables I hadn't bought were included in the recipes that caught my eye. Then I had to make a decision about whether to try to make something with the veggies I had available, or make a quick trip to the local fruit shop and get what was needed. I was of the firm belief that the lack of a variety of vegetables was how frittata and quiche recipes came about: Use what you have and add eggs. No eggs? Nuke it in the microwave, add butter or margarine, sprinkle plenty of pepper, and make it into a vegetable rissole. Did I follow my own advice? No, I just went back to the fish 'n' chips shop and had combo number three or seven.

Living alone teaches you not to try too many products you haven't had before. If you don't like what you have bought, there is no one to help you eat it. My dog would eat most leftovers but wouldn't touch capsicum. Pasta dishes would be devoured, but there would be a neat little pile of capsicum balanced right at the outer edge of the plate. How does a dog do that when it doesn't use their front paws to eat? The plate was otherwise licked clean enough to bypass the dishwasher and go straight back in the cupboard. But of course, I never did that! It was pointless buying a lot of groceries because they went past their "best by" date before I eventually found them in the back of the cupboard. It was annoying, however, to want baked beans on toast for lunch and find out there were none, even in the darker recesses of the cupboards. Somehow scrambled eggs or grilled cheese was not the same, but it was a nutritious meal nevertheless. Tins of soup became somewhat unattractive to open when there was a layer of rust slowly eating into the top of the can. That was the time to really check the "use by" date, no matter how hungry I was.

All this writing about food is making me hungry, so I might just go and see what I can do with the first tin at the front of the shelf. Chickpeas? When on earth did I buy them, and what for? Let my imagination soar, so to speak. Or I can always go and have a combo number five.

Divide and Conquer:
The Lawyers

You might not think so at the time of your divorce, but life can get to be a whole lot better. Divorce changes so many things—some of which we can control and some we can't. Those we can control should be seen as winning posts in the race of life. Those we can't control have to be relegated to the importance of a garden gnome: in that garden in that suburb, that city, that country, how important is a garden gnome?

I love it in the movies, when the offended and usually departing party dramatically flings a suitcase on the well-made and tidy bed and starts to pack. How many of us have pristine, empty suitcases waiting in the wings for this occasion? Specifically, one not filled with jumpers that don't fit anymore or are out of fashion, faded beach towels usually including sand from last year's holiday, and brochures of places one will probably never visit? Not me, that is for sure. My suitcases are like mini storage units, and if I wanted one available for a pack-and-go occasion, I would have to spend half a day emptying some out so I could actually leave.

There is no way that thinking people pack a small suitcase to run away to a new life. Do they even consider what is going to happen to all those clothes they just had to have and are still on hangers with the swing tags attached? Probably not, but at some time in the not too distant future, there will be some crucial item that they have left behind, and then what?

Ring the ex and ask for permission to creep back into what he or she considers his or her house now that you have left? Run the risk of being refused because the locks have been changed to keep you out? Or, even worse, come across the new girlfriend who just happened to find your beautiful, special-occasion lingerie in the bottom drawer behind last year's Christmas cards?

Hell no! No self-respecting person is going to subject herself to any of those scenarios. Take my advice and go buy more of what you need with the credit card your ex doesn't know you still have in your possession. Don't be at the mercy of what is now your ex-life.

For every upside there is always a downside, and for me it was the almost instant ostracising from long-time friends and family that I had known for half my life. I was not naïve enough to believe that I would come out of a separation unscathed, because I had left my first husband when my daughter was less than one year old.

I know that people find it difficult to understand how a marriage of twenty-six years can fall apart, and it is almost as though they think the "failure" might be contagious. Jim and I did not fight publicly, although I was known for making sarcastic comments to him when he really frustrated me or made me angry, but it had gone on for so long that I don't think any of our friends or family thought our marriage had reached the end. I don't think even Jim thought we had arrived at breaking point.

For approximately ten years, there were four couples, including us, who visited each other's houses every six months, and we went away on holidays together at least once a year. The guys of the couples had worked together since being apprentices, so they had the strongest bond, but all the wives got along well, and there were never any problems when we were all together. We shared transportation, costs, food, and drinks, and we even mutually decided on our destination for each weekend away or holiday. It was a great time in our life, and because our children were off our hands, we could go wherever we wanted and for a length of time that suited us.

When I dropped the bombshell of leaving, I was cut adrift from these friends, and the invitations to do things together, as we had for the previous decade, dried up. Before three months had elapsed, I was out in the social desert. I was very grateful that I had my own friends, because they were the only ones that stuck by me and gave me support. I was still the same person, but given that the men of the couples were Jim's friends and the women were the social organisers, my name and address were lost along the way.

It was a similar situation with Jim's family. It was my sister-in-law's birthday at the end of March, and as I had done for the past twenty-seven years, I went across to their home to drop off her gift. Her husband, Jim's brother, met me at the security door and didn't even open it to me. He just spoke to me through the wire, and I was so embarrassed at this rejection that I left her gift on the front doorstep. I never got a chance to see my parents-in-law again, because they lived in Queensland, and it wasn't likely that I would be welcome there, either. The biggest wrench, as far as Jim's family went, was Matthew and his wife, Bonita. I had known Matthew since he was two years old, but within the space of six months we were forever enemies. I haven't spoken to him since we had a very acrimonious telephone conversation in July 2005. He was angry with me because, in his opinion, I treated his father with disrespect by pushing him to move out of the house. He told me that every bit of my behaviour impacted on everyone else, and he asked why I couldn't see that. I said it was none of his business what I did, and I really didn't care what people thought of me. He said that showed how much I had changed, and he didn't like the new Janet. Well, tough.

What no one realised was that I was grieving. I had left behind a marriage, my home that I had put my heart and soul into, my pets that I loved dearly, and some sort of financial security. Had I been a widow and was left alone to cope, I would have been afforded a lot more sympathy and understanding. Being separated and then divorced did not elicit the same responses from people, whether they were family or friends.

Matthew questioned why I had to go through lawyers, and why Jim and I could not come up with a mutually agreeable figure. I told him

I had tried three times with different figures, and Jim had agreed in principle at the time—and then within twenty-four hours he had changed his mind. Matthew said that was because Jim was slow on the uptake and needed time to look at the figures and absorb them.

From this rather protracted conversation with Matthew, it was obvious that it wasn't really about what I had done, but more about how it would impact his life. His father was no longer half of a couple, safely ensconced in another state; he would now require help from outside his marriage. I doubted very much that this was on Matthew's agenda. He said that Jim had no support network like I had. I think Matthew didn't like everything falling into his lap. He didn't like the sudden responsibility for someone whom he thought I was going to worry about for the rest of my life.

Matthew said that it was disrespectful of me to show that I was happy in front of his father. I told him that I *was* happy, and I didn't have to answer to anyone for what I did or where I went. It apparently offended Matthew that I am was going out to the theatre and out with friends, while his father struggled and was short of money. That wasn't my fault! He said that once a figure for settlement was agreed on between Jim and me—and in the meantime I should stop pushing him to settle—it was none of my business where he got the money. If Jim wanted to stay at Pennington, it was none of my business. I believed this was in direct response to my question as to whether Matthew was going to help his father out.

He told me that Jim and I have no negotiating skills, adding "Negotiation is not complete until resolution is reached." He talked like a flying manual. He had downloaded the family law booklet from

Centrelink and admitted that he could not understand any of it. I said that was because he was a pilot, not a lawyer, and maybe he should stick to flying. "Do what you know best, and leave the rest to the experts. That is why I have a family law specialist lawyer."

I was angry and hurt, and I wanted to lash out at anyone who crossed my path. Unfortunately, Matthew did just that when he wanted to know why I had to go to a solicitor, and I said he might not like the answer. I told Matthew that I knew he was cunning and loved money, and that I was not going to sit across the table from him and his father while they screwed me for every last cent. He was horrified that I even thought that.

Why was I being blamed for all this? No separation is 100 per cent one way, and Jim had to take some responsibility for what happened. But at that stage he still didn't know why this happened, even though I had explained to him at least four or five times. Every time I did, he said that was not why. He claimed it was because either he hadn't given me access to his superannuation, or I had too many single friends who encouraged me to leave. Not once did he accept any responsibility for part of what happened.

Matthew mentioned Karen having a go at him the day before, and she had a whole lot of misinformation she was basing her statements on; Matthew assumed that I must have given her that. I told him that my daughter was a grown woman and could quite easily speak for herself. I didn't bash her ear all the time with what was going on, but Jim often rang and poured out his problems to her. I told him Karen was quite entitled to her opinion, and if Matthew had any problems with that, he should contact her—I was not her mouthpiece, nor was she mine. I told him that I raised my child to think for herself, and that was what she was doing. If he didn't like it, he should tell her, not me.

Matthew wanted the family to be the same as it has always been after this is all over. (What planet does he live on?) He wanted his father to be able to go and see Karen, John, and the kids. I told him that Jim went up there for enough time to make and drink a cup of coffee, whirl the kids around his head a few times, and then leave—very quality time, I was sure.

I told him that Jim and I were going to take Cameron out one Saturday a month (when he was little), and that lasted for one outing before Jim went back to the beer bottling and van visit to Gerry at the automotive repair garage, because that was what Jim liked to do on a Saturday. Jade, who was born in June 2004, hasn't been taken out by him once, probably because I wasn't along for the ride. I also told Matthew that Jim had been invited by Karen and John down to the beach house several times, but to date he had not been there. He had also been invited for dinner several times but never stayed long—I suspect because I wasn't there to drive him home after a few beers, and also because he couldn't watch what he wanted on Foxtel.

The end of the conversation (after almost four hours) was neither confrontational nor decisive. He said it would not be a good idea to speak to Bonita yet, because she was also very angry. I told him they mustn't have much to do in their lives if they could keep anger alive for three months. I haven't spoken to him since.

Lawyers are engaged to get their client the best deal possible, but they also have to earn a living. The more consultations that occur—and hence letters to the opposing party—the more dollars that it costs the client. I had already had a taste of that with my first divorce. As this was my second divorce, and I had an intimate knowledge of what it was like to be on the losing team in a property settlement, I wanted the financial arrangements to be equitable for both of us. I decided, against my lawyer's advice, to work out the settlement for Jim and me so that we could both move on with our lives. I didn't hate Jim, but I no longer wanted to be married to him. It was as simple as that. Our assets consisted of a house that was mortgage free, money in the superannuation, a vehicle each with no money owed on either of them, and some shares in each of our names. It wasn't a huge pool of assets, but it was enough for each of us to start a new life with a reasonable amount of security.

I listed our assets and liabilities for the lawyers with the relevant personal details required, and I duly presented this to them at our next meeting. Jim of course took his copy of our agreement to his lawyers and discussed it with them. I agreed to let Jim stay in the house until October 2006, which was almost two years after I left, because I knew he was not happy about moving out and leaving the home he'd had with his first wife, which she'd left behind in 1974. We had some valuations done on the house and agreed on a sale price. Jim had found a townhouse he wanted to buy, so our property was put on the market. Open house viewing times were organised, advertising was discussed, and the process of selling began.

I hadn't been in the house for almost two years, so I had no idea of the condition it was in. Thankfully, my daughter did go and check out what the prospective buyers were going to see, and she reported back to me that it wasn't good. Nobody from the real estate agency had helped Jim with advice on how to present the house and yard to its greatest advantage.

Karen called in to the house on the morning of the last viewing, and she was horrified at the condition of the "housekeeping", or lack of it. She worked really hard and gave Jim instructions on what to do so that it looked cleaner and tidier. He hadn't even made the bed or cleaned up the kitchen; his attitude was that the person was buying the house, not the housework. Presentation was not something that had even crossed his mind.

Many people had gone through the house. On the last viewing day, a prospective buyer came to the front door before the agent was due to arrive. She asked if she could come in and have a look, and Jim readily agreed. She was very happy with the house and thought it would suit their family.

These were the only people who had shown any interest over the six weeks it had been on the market. The price was discussed, but they could only afford five thousand dollars less than the amount Jim and I had agreed on. As our settlement figures were based on the full price, Jim wanted to force them to pay the extra five thousand, with the risk of losing the sale. I told the real estate agent to get the house sold and take the shortfall out of my share, if that was what it took.

Jim went ahead and bought his three-bedroom, double-garage town house; I stayed put in the granny flat behind my mother's house. I had chosen not to buy something because I would have to take out a mortgage, and I was more about lifestyle than working five days a week and constantly battling to pay the bills.

It was my choice at the time, and I didn't regret it. However, seven years after the settlement Jim is living in a town house, and I am now in a rented unit. Did I make the right decision? Only time would tell.

Italy, 2008

17.8.2008—Italy via Hong Kong

I met Dianne when we were working for a medical practice, and we started talking about going on holiday to Italy. We hadn't travelled together before, but we decided to take a chance on going to Italy via Hong Kong, where neither of us had been before. We wanted to design our own tour, so after many Saturday afternoons at her unit, we decided that it would take us thirty-seven days to see all the things we wanted. We chose a date of 17 August 2008 as the first day of our holiday.

I had wanted to go to Italy for a long time, and at last I could tick it off my bucket list. To prepare ourselves for our adventure, we took some classes in tourist Italian so that we could make ourselves understood to a certain extent. Dianne was much better at Italian than I was, and after a few weeks I stopped going to the classes. I thought I would just make do with a lot of sign language.

We arrived at the Seaview Dorset in Hong Kong, where there was absolutely no sea view, and the room made my flat at home look spacious. It didn't matter to us, because we weren't planning on spending much time in it, anyway. We were there to see as much of Hong Kong as we could in our three-day stopover.

The night markets are amazing, but after a while it all looked the same. Water dripped down from the washing—or we hoped it was washing, and not some other effluent. We had an early start for our tour with Virginia Wu, a fast-moving and fast-talking Chinese lady. We crossed Victoria Harbour through a two-kilometre tunnel guaranteed for a hundred years, and it was now thirty-two years old. Note to self: don't go through the tunnel in sixty-eight years. We were amazed to see multi-storey buildings with bamboo scaffolding and shade cloth sides to stop workers falling off the building—yeah, right! No OH&S reps worked here.

For two days we walked all over Kowloon without the benefit of a map, and we didn't get lost. However, day three was a different story. Once we decided to get a taxi, it all went wrong. The driver looked at out hotel card, muttered something in Chinese, and took off. While we were still on Nathan Road, it was okay, but then he did some back-street zigzagging and got to Nim Po Street, which was where Dianne had marked his map as our hotel. We got out of the cab in Nim Po Street, and our hotel was nowhere to be seen. After walking up and down several streets and around the block a few times, we were getting hotter and more frustrated that we couldn't find our hotel—not surprising, because we were about six blocks from it, and our address was the corner of Shanghai Street and Public Square Street. With the help of a nice young local, we eventually made it back to our hotel, completely exhausted by then. I worked out that Dianne didn't have a great sense of direction, and the next time we left our hotel, I made a note of what skyline to head back towards on the way home.

The next day we set off for Rome. When we arrived at the airport, we tried to do an automatic check-in but were unable to because our booking couldn't be located. Went to another section, and after a few phone calls by Crystal, the Cathay Pacific girl, she apologised that they couldn't find the booking, and she asked whether we would mind being upgraded to business class. We were thrilled because we faced a twelve-and-a-half-hour flight overnight.

We were checked in before everyone else, and I was so tired from the Hong Kong heat that all I wanted to do was sleep. The seats reclined almost into a bed, and with the help of an eye mask and earplugs, I went straight to sleep and stayed that way for about seven hours. Dianne couldn't believe that I would miss out on the luxuries of business class and preferred to sleep. Dianne was in the window seat and therefore had to climb over me every time she wanted to go to the toilet, but I didn't hear a thing. We had a lot of turbulence, or so Dianne told me, but it didn't disturb me; I slept on.

When we arrived in Rome, it took about an hour or so to get our bags. Nothing moved very quickly here, unlike in Hong Kong. We checked into our hotel and freshened up. We were ready to start the Italian part of our holiday. We walked to the Spanish Steps in about a half hour, and the views over Rome were beautiful. We had a coffee and continued on to the Trevi Fountain, where we did the typical tourist thing along with thousands of others and threw a coin in the fountain wishing that we would return to Rome. I hoped I would, because I felt so at home there.

We started back for our hotel and then lost our way, but only for a little while. It was hot, we were tired, and I was getting more frustrated by the minute. We finally found a familiar landmark and almost fell in the door of the hotel in relief and exhaustion. This confirmed, for me, that Dianne definitely had no sense of direction. We almost had words earlier on because she'd insisted on going one way, when I sensed that we should go another. After that I took charge of which direction we headed. Oh well, the joys of sharing a holiday.

Our waiter at the Life Restaurant that night was a young man with dark hair and eyes, and he was very good looking, although unfortunately he was young enough to be my son. Dianne was always trying to practice her Italian language, whereas I waved and pointed a lot. We each chose what we wanted to eat, and then Dianne proceeded to order in Italian while the waiter wrote down what we wanted. At the end of our order, Dianne asked in Italian, "Did you get all that?"

He answered, "Sweet as," in English.

I burst out laughing, and Dianne said to him, "Where are you from?"

He replied, "Dee Why, Sydney." Our very Italian-looking waiter was an Aussie just like us, and a long way from home.

The next morning we were walking back to our hotel after a shopping trip, when Dianne suddenly cried out and she said she had a really bad pain in the top of her foot.

We went back to our hotel and applied some ice to her foot, and after a rest we set off again at about 1.40 p.m. to get to the Borghese Villa and Garden. Dianne's foot had started to hurt quite badly, but she struggled on. It was very hot in the rooms of the villa, and it was a long walk home, so we decided to get a cab, which turned out to be the best thing to do because Dianne's foot was getting worse by the minute.

We had a tour booked for the next morning to Vatican City, and by the time we got to the Sistine Chapel, Dianne was hobbling and frightened that someone was going to step on her foot, which was a real fear because it was so crowded. As the tour progressed, the rooms became smaller and the crowds larger and it was becoming quite claustrophobic. We didn't finish the tour and went out a side door to the open-air piazza. We stopped at a cafe for lunch, and Dianne could hardly walk by then, so we got a taxi back to the hotel.

We decided to get a doctor to come to the hotel and see what was wrong with Dianne's foot, because we were to leave for Rimini the next morning. Thank goodness for travel insurance. He didn't think there was a fracture but didn't have the benefit of an X-ray, and he prescribed some Voltaren and painkillers with as much rest as possible. My mother didn't know that the panty liners she'd bought for me to take were used as padding for Dianne's foot.

We were heading for Rimini, over on the coast. We were doing okay and got to the steps of the train, which were steep and started off about sixty centimetres from the platform. This was our first experience of Italian trains. Dianne's foot was padded underneath with the panty liners and then firmly strapped into her sneakers.

I helped Dianne in with her bag, and then this guy in dark pants and a blue shirt (who was apparently on the train) almost pushed Dianne out of the way and started talking loudly to a group of six people who were standing behind me. They pushed past, and he grabbed their bags and proceeded to load them up onto the racks above their seats. I then went to lift my bag on, and Dianne went to help me, when the man reappeared and went off down the carriage with our bags. He virtually threw them up on the rack above our seats and then indicated we should give him a tip. The tip I would have like to give him was, "Piss off." He had no chance of a tip once he had pushed Dianne out of the way and then put six people in front of us. In your dreams, buddy.

When we had to change trains at Bologna, we had to get our twenty-kilogram cases out of the rack above our seat. I stood on the seat to get the cases down, and I was okay for most of the time until the first case suddenly came over the edge of the rack and hit the floor. Luckily it missed me on the way down, but I was holding onto one of the handles, and the force of the bag dropping pitched me forward into the glass partition at the entrance to our seats. I successfully made a fool of myself in front of a carriage full of people, but I wouldn't have put the cases up there in the first place.

We changed trains at Bologna by negotiating several stairways. That was definitely not fun. It was dangerous to let anyone help with one's bags because one may never see the person or the bags again. Then the gypsies started coming through the train. First there was a woman with a baby, then a guy handing out bits of paper for some obscure reason, then a guy with a card and a toy. The things to do was avoid eye contact and don't speak, because they then knew we were not Italian and would keep pestering us.

We arrived in Rimini without mishap and caught a taxi to our hotel. We had a nice little terrace off the room, but they had made the twin beds into one giant bed. I planned to get some sheets later and make up the couch into a bed for me. It didn't happen because nobody knew for what we were actually asking. If I had known the phrase "non-matrimoniale" meant not married, it would have helped.

We planned to go by bus to San Marino the next day, but first I had to do my washing in the bidet. I had to improvise. I was in absolute agony in a bookstore full of my favourite authors, and I couldn't buy anything because they were all in Italian! Bugger! The only thing that had any English in it was Shakespeare's Twelfth Night. Somehow I don't think it would have been readily translated into Italian, but I wasn't that desperate for a read.

The sheets never did arrive, but we took one off the bed, and I slept on the couch, which was actually quite comfortable because I was used to sleeping in a single bed. We turned off the air conditioner and put the security screen down on the door. Good night, Rimini.

The taxi dropped us in Rimini at the bus stop for San Marino. We tried to buy bus tickets where it had a bus sign—as per the instructions at the bus stop—but the shop didn't sell tickets for the San Marino bus, of course. About two minutes before the bus arrived, a seriously senior citizen roared up on a motorbike, parked on the footpath, and started selling tickets. Go figure. The trick was that we had to come back on the same bus line, even though two go to the same place, and if we didn't get the right bus, it meant being stranded in San Marino, which was about forty-five minutes up in the mountains from Rimini. No taxis went up there.

The next day was 25 August—my thirtieth wedding anniversary if I had remained with Jim. I preferred to be single and in Italy.

We arrived at the train station the next morning and had eighteen minutes to change trains for Venice. Again we did the two-person bag shuffle, and as we went downstairs to validate our ticket, we found we had to go back up to the platform we had just left. This wasn't doing Dianne's sore foot much good, but that's Italy for you.

After checking into our hotel, we walked over the Rialto Bridge and crossed to the other side of the Grand Canal. It was about 7.00 p.m., and the setting sun was reflected on the buildings, making them a beautiful, soft, golden pink colour. I don't think I have ever seen anything quite so lovely. We decided to have a gondola ride, because it was a beautiful night, and there wasn't much traffic on the canal. It was absolutely fabulous. One more thing crossed off the bucket list.

The next morning, as we walked around Venice, I had observed that the people selling copy handbags put their wares out on a large white sheet, and I assumed that it was to keep the bags clean until they were sold. However, as we were walking along the canal, there was a lot of noise coming from one of the alleys that ran at right angles to the canal. Quick as a wink, a young man picked up the four corners of the sheet and slung it and the bags it contained over his shoulder, disappearing up another alley. Obviously the sheet served more than one purpose when one was trying to sell illegal goods.

I asked Dianne to stop into a coffee shop because I had to use the toilet. The queue for the ladies was quite long, so when a man came out of the gents, the waiter told me to go in instead of waiting for the ladies to be vacant. I had never actually had to squat over a urinal before, but there was a first time for everything. I wish I had a photo of the look on the face of the guy waiting to go in.

The bloody bell near our bed and breakfast rang seventy-five times in one session—what were they doing? We asked several Venetians what the bell was for, but nobody seemed to know. Some things were simply lost in history and translation.

At Murano Island our first stop was at a glass blowing factory—with shop of course, through which we had to enter and leave. Then it was on to Burano, where they still made lace by hand. Each person specialised in a particular stitch, so it could take seven to ten people to make one article. Our next and last stop was Torcello, featuring old ruins, an old church, souvenirs, and cold drinks—same old, same old.

We were supposed to be back at the boat at 12.20, but we misjudged it by less than five minutes, and they were just about to leave. We couldn't walk quickly because Dianne's foot was really paining. They put their gangway back down again, and we hurried on board while the tour woman admonished us in a shrill voice for being "very late". Several of the passengers were displeased, because they had to start another tour as soon as we got back to Venice, and some English passengers muttered something about "bloody Australians".

We were due to leave Venice for Milan, but the day didn't start out well because we missed our train by about four minutes and had to buy more tickets. Because my case was on four wheels and was out in the corridor, when some of the other bags were moved, it took off by itself down the corridor after one of the passengers. It was quite funny to watch a tourist trying to outrun a moving suitcase.

We were off to Lake Como by coach, and then a ferry would take us to Bellagio, a small village about two hours by boat. George Clooney wasn't home at the time, unfortunately, but his home was pointed out to us. The next part of the journey was from Milan to Monterosso by train. Thank goodness there were escalators. There were two trains leaving at 8.10 a.m. from two different platforms, and neither showed our destination. I saw a railway employee pushing along a sign with "Assistance—Ask Me" written on it, but when I approached him, he wouldn't acknowledge my existence until he finally stopped where he was stationed at a booth.

After we struggled with our bags down the cobbled streets of the town, Dianne went to find Franca Maria, who owned the flat we were to stay in, and it wasn't long before we settled in. I did some washing and went to hang it outside the window on their funny clotheslines that were operated by ropes and pulleys. It dripped down onto the staff going in and out of the restaurant downstairs, which I hadn't noticed, so I had to take it off the line when the restaurant owner abused me in Italian. My grasp of Italian was not that great, but believe me, he managed to get the message across. A raised and shaken fist is understandable in any language.

We had decided to go on a ferry trip to Portovenere in the afternoon. In Italy the printed timetable was merely a guide to what may be available, and when—it was definitely not carved in stone. However, we found out that the last ferry listed for the return trip didn't actually return. In reality, the last ferry returned to some other port for the night. This was a fairly handy piece of information if one was ten kilometres from where one was staying. We decided to get an earlier ferry that might return us to our embarkation point. One could hope. Portovenere was a lovely little town, and we caught the last ferry back, but it was not the one listed as the last ferry on the timetable. It was very confusing for the average Joe Tourist.

Our five-day stay was up, and we had to pay Franca Maria for our room because we were leaving early the next morning for the trip to Florence. We rang the bell where she lived but got no response, so we waited a few minutes more. Some ladies appeared who only spoke Italian, and we pantomimed that we wanted to pay for our room, so they took us across to someone who could speak English and explained to them what we were trying to do. They scattered in all directions looking for Franca Maria. The word must have gotten through, because she came to the flat and asked Dianne to go to her place at about 8.30. The Italian version of the Aussie bush telegraph worked perfectly.

It was time to leave Cinque Terre for Florence. Earlier we had noticed a lift up to the platform, but of course on the day my bags were the heaviest, my back was sore, and Dianne's foot ached, we had to walk up a hill to the station and drag our bags up the steps because the lift was having an "off day". Of course.

When we were getting on the train at Pisa for Florence, a young woman with a baby but no purse or baggage got on with us and followed Dianne down the steps and into the lower carriage. Two young teenagers stood between the doorway to the lower landing and me, effectively preventing Dianne and I from being together. We were the only people in the carriage, and the lady with the baby went to sit down near Dianne's case. Dianne had a firm hold on her backpack and told the woman to move. We had been warned about the gypsies and how quick they were to relieve people of their baggage. It was definitely a scam, and fortunately it didn't work. We had finally had our "gypsy experience" that everyone talked about, and we had survived.

We got into Florence, had lunch at a local café, and then walked across the Ponte Vecchio, the bling capital of the world. There was every sort of jewellery the heart could desire, but it was an assault on the eyes because everything was jammed together, and no single piece had a chance to stand out. Oh well, it didn't cost anything to look.

Our tour in the Accademia was pre-booked, and it was very informative and interesting. I couldn't believe how many people used their mobile phones to take pictures when there were signs everywhere saying no photos, but the guards didn't do anything about it, so the people kept doing it. One guy was even taking a video. Uffizzi Gallery was on our tour list for the next day. I bought a book about the art in Florence, which I planned to send home because it was very heavy. I then assisted the local economy by buying some handmade paper and notebooks.

We were heading off for our self-guided walking tour of Tuscany. Dianne had researched it before we left Sydney, and according to the instructions it was "easy walking and well marked". We were too early for the train to Chiusi, but we were being met in Montalcino and didn't want to be late. After an uneventful train ride from Florence to Chiusi, we were met by Mario, who brought us to the Il Giglio hotel, which was ancient. We were on the second floor and had a fantastic view from the window.

Montalcino to Castelnuove del Abate was the first real day of our walk through Tuscany. With bags packed and breakfast over, we were ready to leave at 9.30. We asked the guy on the desk how to exit the town so we could start the first part of our walk according to our instructions. He said, "Left and then left again," which we did . . . and we came to the first problem. We thought we were on the wrong road, even though we were below the stadium, but we couldn't see the roundabout. Back up the road we went until we took the second left and took the road on the right, which turned out to be correct. We didn't even manage to exit the first town correctly—not an encouraging start to our six-day walk.

We found the roundabout and the bar beside it where we were to turn right. The instructions said there was a police station on the corner and a map of the walk on a pole, neither of which we could see. We walked about a hundred metres down the road but weren't confident we were in the right place, even though the street names matched. Back we went, to where we had turned right beside the bar. There was a map on a post, but of course it was facing the wrong way, and we couldn't see it. Back down the road we headed, and we eventually started our 12.5-kilometre, 2.5-hour walk, which was the distance and time required to complete this first day according to Hidden Italy, who had produced the instructions. So far it had taken us almost 1.5 hours just to get to the starting point. It was going to be a long day.

We followed this track down until we got to a detour; a farmer had fenced off this part of the property to extend his vineyard and enclose his land, which was fair enough, but Hidden Italy hadn't quite caught up with this change. The next part of the instructions was as the terrain encountered, and then we had to go in the direction of a "small, rickety, wooden arrow pointing to Sant Antimo". Very accurate description. We were then on a track through thick forest for "about ten minutes". Well, there were so many loose, dry leaves on the track that our pace was slowed down considerably. I had to keep my eyes on where I was putting my feet and making sure I didn't slip. The so-called handrail was almost on the ground because it had fallen over or someone had knocked it down. We eventually got down to the "stream" and found a gravel road where we were to go left, but there was no red and white marker, just a blue and yellow one, so we weren't sure which way to go. We went downhill for a while, but again we couldn't see any red and white markers. I offered to go back up to where the track split, and I then saw a red and white marker on a tree trunk, hidden by shrubs about two metres from the ground. We were back on track but had already used up two hours, and we were hardly out of sight from where we started.

The farmhouse at the T-intersection, called Prata, only had half of its sign visible, and we guessed to go down the left side of it. Amazingly we guessed correctly. This should be a total walk so far of forty metres. We came to another T-intersection of our dirt road and an asphalt road. We walked up this to find the sign indicating Tavernelle to the right. Well, we could see a whole lot of signs, but we couldn't see the dirt track on the left because it was actually hidden behind a whole lot of trucks parked there. Once we found the track, we followed this until we reached an asphalt road, which we had to cross, and then we continued up another hill in the hot sun. By now it was three and a half hours since we started, and according to our instructions, this part should have only taken one hour.

We found the road to the left for Villa a Tolli, where it said 8.7 kilometres on the sign, and we hoped it wasn't anywhere near that distance. We had a break, sitting on a wall just down from Podere Cocco, the highest point of the walk at 610 metres. It was supposed to take one hour and thirty minutes to this point, but we had been walking for over four hours. This was not going well.

We then had to take a detour around La Magia Vineyard and go down a path that Hidden Italy described as "a bit rough". It was a section of forest that had been graded at some previous time, and most of the width of the "road" consisted of boulders ranging from the size of tennis balls to soccer balls. The stones were really loose and very hard to walk on safely. The edges were not much better because they sloped to the centre and were slippery as well. We were not having fun and had just about had enough. This was not what we expected from the description in the blurb about "graded country roads". It was now almost five hours since we had started, and we really didn't have any idea how much longer it was going to take to reach our destination.

Dianne took a photo of the terrain to send to Simon of Hidden Italy when we got back. We were very disappointed, and Dianne and I seriously considered pulling out of the next day's walk because our legs and thighs were so sore from that ridiculously rocky part of the track. Also, Dianne's foot was giving her some pain, so we decided to rest up the next day. This day's walking had actually taken six hours, which was three and a half hours more than indicated on our instructions.

According to Anna, the tour company's representative whom we managed to contact by mobile phone, day three from San Antimo to San Quirico d'Orcia was a longer walk. She did warn us that if we got near the railway (more than halfway), they would not be able to get us out if we were too tired to go on. That was enough for me. We agreed to rest up and continue the day after. Getting lost in Italy may sound romantic, but we were two ladies over sixty, and we were not having a romance with each other.

We decided to start day four earlier because we had about twelve kilometres to cover, as advised by the walking guide, but given our experience so far, we weren't at all sure how long it would take. We went to a recommended shop for cheese, salami, and bread, all locally produced, for our lunch later on in the day. Dianne and I also bought two five-hundred-millilitre bottles of water each and were on our way by 10.00 a.m.

The instructions on our sheet from Hidden Italy seemed quite clear, and we easily found the first turn off to our right. We were on our way and it was already hot. We tramped along the road, and Dianne had washed out her nightie and slung it over her backpack to dry. When we got out of sight of the town, she tied it onto her hat so that it would flap in the wind and dry. It looked weird but was successful. I didn't look much better holding up an umbrella to keep the sun off my head. I hate hats, and this was a better option for me.

After we found the farm Costigeato, we turned right. About halfway down the hill, Dianne said she felt dizzy, so we decided to stop under a tree. Little did we know this would be the last shade for quite a while. It was about 12.40 p.m., so we decided to have lunch.

There didn't seem to be anyone at the farmhouses that we passed, but as we came to the top of yet another hill, Dianne was struggling with the heat quite a bit more than I was. I was using my umbrella as a sort of portable shade, and it was keeping the sun off most of my body, except my legs. I also had on shorts, sandals, and a sleeveless top; whereas Dianne had a short-sleeved top and long pants with socks, and she wore sneakers because of her sore foot. Dianne had a hat on, but her body was in the sun, which was making her quite hot. We had almost exhausted our water supply, but we still had a long way to go to reach Pienza. There was a house just a little way down the hill with washing on the line, so I took two of our bottles to see if we could get them refilled with water. There was a man resting in a hammock, and he was kind enough to fill them for me. I was very grateful.

By 3.15 we decided to send a text message to Anna, to see if she could arrange for someone to come and collect us, because Dianne was really struggling physically. By 3.45 we hadn't heard from her, but with a bit more water on board we decided to try to get to Pienza under our own steam. I figured that God helped those that helped themselves, and there didn't seem to be any help coming from the Hidden Italy representative anytime soon.

We could see the town and guessed it would probably take about an hour to get there. As we started walking again, I saw a truck drive through a gateway. From the illustrations on the side, it would seem to be a fruit and vegetable business. I walked up to the door of the house and asked if we could buy some water. I think the two Euros I paid was the best money spent on the trip, and it helped to rehydrate us for the rest of the journey into Pienza.

We kept walking slowly towards Pienza and found a thirteenth-century church, where we went in and sat in the cool shade. Although I was not particularly religious, I lit a candle for the people who had helped us that day, because if they hadn't been home, I didn't know what we would have done. We were both dehydrated, Dianne more so than me because she was a bit light-headed, and her blood pressure was up as well.

We pressed on, and eventually at about 4.45, we arrived in Pienza and almost collapsed in the foyer of the hotel. A pleasant surprise awaited us because our bags were already in our room, and there was a lift. This was a great end to a very hard day. I fell on the bed and slept for an hour because dinner wasn't until 7.30.

We had decided we wouldn't walk on Thursday because of the expected high temperatures and the distance of the walk, which was about sixteen kilometres. Enough was enough, and I never wanted to feel that worried about getting water ever again. I wondered afterwards when and even if the alarm would have been raised that we hadn't arrived at Pienza, and whether anyone would have gone looking for us.

The host and his wife at our next hotel were charming and welcoming. It was just like living in their home. Our bed was made up as a double, and we asked that it be changed to two singles. I had learned the phrase "non-matrimoniale" by then. I think that the host may have forgotten that he was matrimoniale because he followed Dianne up onto the roof terrace and firmly kissed her on the lips. It shocked her to her shoes, and she was wary of him after that.

We were to go to a very nice local restaurant that night, and I wanted to wear my sandals, but the stony roads were so treacherous for high heels that I decided to wear something more appropriate for the terrain. It was a steep hill down to the restaurant, and of course that meant a steep hill up coming back, along with some alcohol on board—not a good idea. We had a beautiful meal and felt confident enough to take a shortcut home, making it safely back to the hotel. We decided that we had ticked "walking through Tuscany" firmly off our bucket list.

We returned to Rome for the last part of our holiday, and after settling into our hotel, we went in search of dinner. We had dinner at Life Restaurant, and halfway through dinner it started to rain. Out of the night appeared this young Negro man with a basket full of umbrellas for sale. Now that was being really entrepreneurial. It was shopping, shopping, and more shopping, broken up only by eating and drinking, but at least we walked everywhere, so that should offset some of the last two items.

It is my dream to go back to Italy some day; maybe those coins thrown into the Trevi Fountain will work.

When we arrived back in Sydney, my daughter and grandchildren were there to meet me with balloons and a big sign. It was so nice to be home. I had to fast-track my jet lag because it was Cameron's birthday

party the next day. He had put it off for a week when I booked my
trip, and I was hoping it wouldn't rain and spoil it for him. I had
asked Cameron if he would mind changing the date of his party until
I got back from my holiday, and he said it was okay with him. Mum
had already had a go at me before I left that I should get my priorities
right and be back in time for Cameron's birthday, instead of two days
later. I told her that he was with the most important people, his dad,
mum, and sister, and that she should mind her own business.

Help—My House Is Being Eaten!

I had been living in the granny flat for almost four years, and things were getting more difficult between Mum and me. We had never had a good relationship but managed okay when we lived in two different postcodes. Sharing the same yard, garage, and driveway was a recipe for a bit of nastiness on her part. There was constant criticism about when I used the washing machine, when I hung out the washing, when I brought the washing in, and so on. It was all such rubbish and didn't impact on her at all, but she couldn't keep quiet and have a peaceful life. She knew every bit of mail I got and when any friends came to visit, but more important (to her) was when they left.

The family spent Christmas 2008 at my daughter's holiday home, down on the south coast of NSW. I had learned from my previous experiences of there being three generations in one household, even for a limited time, that there would be difficulties. Include my mother as one of those generations, and it was doomed to failure.

I enjoyed being with Karen, John, and my two grandchildren, Cameron and Jade. We loved going down the beach, splashing around in the rock pools, and generally enjoying the holiday atmosphere. Karen had bought me three books for Christmas because she knew I love to read; however, I didn't think I had ever seen my mother with a book in her hands, and certainly not the one *How to Win Friends and Influence People.*

There are two sorts of people when it comes to books. There are those who read, and those who don't because they see reading as a waste of time. I was in the first category, and my mother was very firmly in the second. Not being one to delay voicing an opinion, she pointed out that I had my head in a book every chance I got. My reply was that I was on holidays, didn't read at the table, and didn't read when someone is speaking to me, but I did read when I have a comfortable chair and time to spare. I also asked her how it affected her, exactly.

I had just about had enough of her, so I told her she was my mother not my keeper, and she should worry about what she was doing with her time and not be concerned with what I did with mine. She didn't even like it when I sat with Cameron and Jade, painting or playing a game.

She had an opinion on everything and everyone, even without any knowledge to back it up. She was critical about people and the way they ran their lives, but if someone turned the tables on her, she would be furious. It must be hard, to be perfect in such an imperfect world. She also told me I drank too much, so I agreed with her. That gave me about ten minutes peace, until she started on about how it will kill me. Yes, it probably would, but I might die in gaol for murdering her in the meantime. She was such hard work! I let her carry on with her tirade and walked away from her. No audience meant no point.

When the end of 2008 arrived, I was very glad because it had not been a happy year for lots of people, with financial worries topping the list. My finances had been hit as well, but not as hard as some who had lost their home, business, or life savings. New Year's was traditionally a time for making resolutions to change one's life, lose weight, stop drinking, get more exercise, grow taller, or other silly things people knew in their hearts were not going to happen. I really had no clue what I was going to do with the rest of my life, and I had hit a real flat spot. I wasn't happy with the job I was doing, I didn't like that Mum knew everything about my life, and I thought it was about time I worked out a plan. I was sixty-three years old and living in less than happy circumstances. I wondered where the last forty years had gone since I'd left that address a hopeful, young woman marrying for the first time and starting a new life.

The time Dianne and I had spent planning our wonderful Italian holiday had left a big hole to fill when the trip was behind me. I knew that I had to get some form of exercise regimen happening and cut down on my drinking, this latter issue being a constant battle for me.

I had to be fairly alert each day because I had started a new job working in the office of a friend I had known for about ten years.

It was close to home and the hours were fairly flexible, so it suited me in some ways. On the downside was the reduced pay per hour, and, because I was employed on a casual basis, the uncertainty of my weekly income. It was a huge learning curve, and even though I had computer skills, they did not exactly cover what I needed to know for his work.

I had worked in the medical field for most of my working life and was not really up to speed with the Internet, so that made it a difficult job for me. Also he wasn't the nicest person to work for, at that time as he was going through some personal issues as well. I didn't like working by myself because I found it hard to stay motivated, but I had chosen to do this job, so I had to get on with it.

I couldn't afford to move somewhere else without dipping into my savings, but I thought that if I could redecorate the flat and make it more mine, than a patchwork of other people's decorating preferences, then I could perhaps settle down and put up with my mother and her lack of social skills.

Added to this, Mum was quite happy to use up whatever spare hours I had to take her here and there; this also allowed her to criticise my driving, my sense of direction, and anything else she could think of. It was a wonder I bothered to go back and collect her from friends or family after a visit. It was very tempting to let them put up with her for a while longer until her "Sweet Doreen" façade melted with the afternoon sun, and they got to see the real person.

I now had a regular income, but it was certainly not enough to take on a major refurbishment, even though the flat was quite small, so

I asked my son-in-law if he thought tiling the top floor would be an expensive job. On a sunny Saturday morning in February 2009 my son-in-law and grandson arrived at the flat to talk about just tiling the top floor, which I thought might improve the overall appearance. Over a cuppa, John and I decided that if we were going to do this renovation of the top floor, we might as well continue downstairs as well. This meant that I could have a bedroom and bathroom downstairs with a toilet (oh, joy—no more dashes across the backyard in the rain). The top floor would be the kitchen, living area, lounge, and a desk for my computer.

The downside of this renovation would be that I would have to live in Mum's house for ten weeks, and that didn't thrill either of us, but she did agree that I could move in. I had the use of Dad's old bedroom and one other room, so that I could store my more easily damaged belongings such as the television and CD player. With the exception of my clothes and toiletries, everything else was packed into cardboard boxes and stored under the kitchen. It was damp, but I put carpet over the old vinyl on the floor and hoped it would all emerge intact and without a coating of blue mould. For some inexplicable reason, I wasn't allowed to store anything in her garage, but I suspect that it may have made it easier for me.

And so the demolition began, with John the foreman and Cameron his able apprentice. They came every Saturday and Sunday for three months to do this for me. They worked so hard and spent many hours removing thousands of nails from the floors and walls. Cameron constantly borrowed John's pinch bar, and when John wanted it back, he told his dad to get his own because he was having too much fun to hand it over.

Cameron had his own toolbox with wheels, and it accompanied him every time he came to do some work. My daughter and my four-year-old granddaughter also came over and helped for hours on end. The kids worked so hard carrying all the rubbish up to the front yard, which was a difficult exercise in itself, and throwing it into two skips. It was hard work and very dirty, but they kept at it. I was so proud of them and the work they did.

When the flat was stripped back to the bare bones of its structure, it was revealed in all its home handyman constructed glory. Straight, square, or level were obviously foreign concepts to my father when he built this building, which was originally a garage back in the 1950s.

Rats behind the sandstone wall downstairs were mummified now because they had been there so long. We discovered termites behind the wardrobe upstairs when we pulled it off the wall. Cockroaches scurried away or flew, if they were the big, brown, shiny ones. Millions of ants, the small black and tenacious species, crept around at all hours of the day and night. No matter what we sprayed, they or their nest mates returned overnight to find their way to any crumbs left behind by the last lot of tradesmen. I felt that we had uncovered a whole new world of subterranean creatures that had shared my abode for five years, and I was never aware of their comings and goings—or in the case of the rats, their staying.

The upstairs walls of the flat were made of recycled timber that Dad had picked up from wherever he happened to see it. Back in the 1950s, he had a flat-bed truck, so long lengths of timber from buildings or wharves being demolished were perfect. This was long before Jack Mundey came along and saved The Rocks from destruction. Dad didn't know it then, but the creosote on some of the collected timbers was the only thing that kept the termites from eating away the whole top storey and burying me under it.

Dad's garage was always the resting place for bikes without chains, chairs with one leg missing, and anything else he deemed would one day be useful. Define "useful", I say. Nothing left on the side of the road was safe from Dad and his flat-bed truck. When we had to clean it out to try to fit two cars in, it was a nightmare of gigantic proportions.

One of Dad's favourite sayings was, "There are the quick and the dead," and unfortunately he now qualified on both counts. He was ahead of his time in recycling, but for Dad it was more about saving money than the environment. The thirty-centimetre-thick sandstone blocks for the downstairs walls had been cut by hand from his property and those unoccupied blocks around us. Not many of our close neighbours ever had the problem of ridding their properties of unwanted sandstone once Dad had finished the lower level of the property with retaining walls and the bottom level of the flat.

The stone walls downstairs did not have surfaces that were anywhere near smooth. The walls were lined with Masonite, which could be bent quite easily, so Dad's idea of keeping it all firm was to get bigger nails and bang them in harder. However, in 2009 when these same studs and noggins had the Masonite removed and ready to be covered in plasterboard, underneath, which was just a dab of glue, there were a lot of problems. It was a real challenge for Louie, the plasterer, and it cost me another 50 per cent for an aggravation fee.

Everything we uncovered seemed to add to the ever-increasing estimate for the renovation. The poor guy who installed the kitchen had to cope with a tiled floor that fell away to one side, walls that weren't straight, and a window that was out of square. He certainly earned his dollars on that one.

I had a great time deciding on colours, patterns, kitchen fit out, and appliances. The site was very difficult, with most materials having to be brought down the side of the house and across the backyard. There was no opportunity to use any sort of mechanical help because there was no access through the garage, so we did it the hard way, with the appropriate increase in costs.

I had to take thirty thousand dollars out of my superannuation to pay for everything, but it was well and truly worth it. I had somewhere clean, bright, and pest-free to live with new furniture and an indoor toilet. Sometimes it is the little things that make people the happiest.

By the end of ten weeks, things were more than a little tense between Mum and me, and I felt that she was as glad to see me move out of her house, as I was glad to go. At least my dog could be kept confined with me and not under her house "knocking things over and making a noise".

The Dating Game

I t'd been some thirty-five years since I was on the singles scene, and things had changed enormously since then. The usual meeting places in 1974 were dances, hotels, or clubs, when I could actually carry on a conversation with the person I was interested in; the level of the music allowed me to do that.

Also, dancing was a lot more upfront and personal than it is now, with the partners holding each other while they waltzed, tangoed, or stepped the barn dance. Alcohol was served, of course, but the choices were much more limited than they are now. Mostly the guys drank beer and the girls had a drink such as vodka and orange, or wine. One dreadful drink I remember was called Pimms, and it was so sweet that it was hard to digest; usually it was decorated with cucumber and other assorted fruits or vegetables around the top of the glass. It looked much better than it actually tasted.

There was no breathalyser, and the amount of alcohol consumed was only limited by how much money the guys had in their pockets. It was the usual thing for the man to ask the lady if she would like a drink. Girls hardly ever paid for their own drinks, except maybe one to start the night off before being noticed by a guy. Date-rape drugs had not been invented, and getting tipsy wasn't part of the night's entertainment. The venues were usually auditoriums in the local council chambers, with beautifully polished floors and a stage where the band or orchestra played. The lighting was quite bright, and one could actually see one's partner. The music was loud enough to dance to but not so deafening that one couldn't hold a conversation. The dances usually started about 7.00 p.m. and finished by 11.00 because all "good" girls should be in bed—by themselves—no later than 1.00 a.m.

I divorced Jim in March 2007, so by the time 2009 rolled around, I thought I would try Internet dating. So much had changed about the dating scene. I had to get some inside information from friends who had been successful in finding a partner, although sometimes for a disappointingly short time. I was advised about serial daters, people who are on several different Internet sites. There was some juicy information on guys whom friends had been out with, what they were like in bed (the guy, that is), and even an astonishing amount of information about the anatomy hidden from view by jeans. Too much information! I was starting to get a bit scared by a few of these conversations, and it became even more interesting sitting in front of a computer screen and scrolling down the pages of the likely, the dodgy, and the married. I was under the impression that the people who went on these websites to try to meet someone were single. Apparently not so; there were quite a number of these "Oh, I forgot I had a wife" people.

A friend tried speed dating, and that was another interesting concept of how to meet someone. This night was for singles only—fairly specific, I thought. She met a man, who seemed quite nice, and he ticked her card and she ticked his, so they organised to meet. A week or so later, they got together for coffee, and she asked him, "If we went out and I wanted to come back to you place, would that be a problem?" His answer absolutely floored her. "Well, you could, but my wife wouldn't like it." What a cheek!

I really just wanted a male to share a social life with, and I was quite upfront about that on my profile. I had no intention of moving in with someone, and I certainly did not want to get married again. I didn't necessarily want to meet the man's family or get invited to birthday parties.

I first tried RSVP, which was a well-known dating site, and also eHarmony, just to widen the net a little. I found a photo of myself that was reasonably flattering and up to date, and I posted it on the two sites. Then I had to come up with an interesting overview of who and what I was, what I was expecting from a relationship, and more. I tried to be honest about my expectations and what type of person I am. However, after a few contacts with the opposite sex, albeit it over the Internet, I worked out that not everyone was truthful, and in some cases they were quite wide of the mark.

The photos people posted on the dating sites were sometimes years out of date, and it was really interesting that some men thought it is attractive to have a photo in their worst T-shirt and shorts holding a stubby of beer up to the camera with a look on their face that gave me the impression they might have had a few too many. However, I supposed it all depended on the fish they were trying to catch.

I had a friend who found her other half on the Internet, and they are still together six years later. They live in two separate addresses, and maybe that is part of the success of their relationship. They are only together when they actually want to be.

The age of a woman specified by men on the websites is very interesting. Men in their fifties want a woman thirty-five or older; men in their sixties (my age group) want someone forty-five or older. By the time you get to a man wanting a woman in their sixties, you are dealing with men in the eighty-plus range. Not quite what I had in mind. No wonder women lied about their age!

I didn't want a man whom I have to look after, or a man who just wanted to go to the footy or hang around in a club. I want to share time, going out to dinner, getting to know them by talking, going to see a movie that interested us both, and spending time in the great outdoors, walking and doing things together. However, I was instantly suspicious about those who wanted to go moonlight walking on a beach. Did that mean ugly women could apply?

Unfortunately, it would appear that not many men shared my ideas of spending time together. I met one lovely man, and we had lunch at a club about halfway between our addresses. However, he had only been widowed for about nine months and was still in the grieving process. He basically wanted someone to fill the void his wife had left, and I could imagine how thrilled his children would have been about that.

I went to a local club to see a show with some friends, and a man sat alone in the only spare seat at our table. He looked rather nice, seemed to enjoy the show, and we all had a bit of a chat in the interval. He then went downstairs to play the poker machines. I was rather taken with him and decided I would go and find him. I usually carried a small notebook in my purse, not for giving my details to men but more for reminding me of what I have to do.

I went down to where the poker machines were located and found him. I walked up to him, tapped him on the shoulder, and said, "I don't usually do this sort of thing, but you look rather nice, and I was wondering if you would like to meet up for a coffee sometime." I handed him a piece of paper with just my first name and mobile number on it. He looked taken aback but accepted the proffered number. A few days later, he phoned me and introduced himself, and we met for dinner the next weekend.

I felt quite safe with him, and a week or so later I phoned and asked him if he would like to come to my home for a meal. He arrived on time with a bottle of wine—all good so far. Then he brought out three photo albums with travel photos, totalling about one thousand images. Well the wine was drunk, the dinner was burned, and I had never been so bored in my life. I didn't see him again.

I met up with another man at a restaurant, again about halfway between our addresses, and we seemed to get along quite well while we were having dinner. He walked me back to my car and asked if he could sit there with me for a while. I was a bit wary because this dating scene was so new to me, and back in the seventies it was the guy in the driver's seat, not the girl. Oh well, times had changed. He asked me if he could give me a kiss, and I said okay, but then it went a bit too far for my comfort zone. I wasn't ready for tonsil hockey and said that I had to get home, and we left it at that. He rang me again, and I agreed to go to the movies with him. Again he walked me to my car but this time he thought that diving down my top with his sweaty hands was okay. He soon found out it wasn't okay with me. I had paid for my own movie ticket, and I wasn't on the menu as dessert, thanks very much. I had already explained that I wasn't interested in a physical relationship, so we parted company.

Back to the Internet, to try again. Why did people not believe me when I said that I just wanted companionship? There were so many other issues that were part of the dating scene now, even if I was a senior person. There was no way that one could tell whether this person was married, whether he was the person he said he was, whether he lived where he said, or how many other people he was dating. If the relationship became physical, which most of them seemed to expect, how much did body image come into it? Mobile phones and emails turned the dating scene on its head. One could be anywhere in the world and say one was somewhere around the corner.

What about the guys who were impotent? Do they not get to the intimate bit, borrow some Viagra from a friend, or not bother even putting their face up on the screen? The mind might be willing, but would the body be able? I worked for urologists, so I knew how many men had problems in the undies area.

People over sixty were not all that attractive undressed, so how was this managed? There was an article in the paper titled "How to Look

Good Naked". Were they kidding? I would have to go around and remove half of the light globes, and change the rest to twenty-five watts, to stand any sort of chance to look "good". It crossed my mind that hiding the man's glasses would also help. It was obvious that gravity had visited me and pulled my breasts and belly into a more downward-facing position, but the thought of baring all before a male made me quake in my shoes—or it wouldn't, because I wouldn't be wearing any shoes!

What did one do about the possibility of STDs? Did I pack my own choice of condoms? Who supplied the Viagra, assuming it was required? Who paid for what, now that we had equality? If the man paid for my meal and drinks, did this entitle him to sex? Were there date rapes in the senior age group? What if the sex was awful? It was a minefield!

And last but not least, what did the family think about it? Were they happy you are trying to find someone, or horrified that Grandma goes out on dates with men they haven't met? What if Grandma gets married again? What if Grandma moves away with her new love? But then again, how much say should the family have?

I did eventually meet a nice man who was about seven years older than I was. He wanted the same sort of friendship that I did, and he was quite honest about it. For about eighteen months, we went out at least once or twice a week, but then he became interested in "what the Muslims were doing to this country", and I got tired of listening to him go on about it. It consumed his life, and everything he sent me in email was about this subject. I finally decided that we were not on the same page anymore, and I asked him to stop contacting me.

That was two years ago now, and I haven't bothered with Internet dating since.

I wanted companionship, someone with whom I could go for walks, go see movies, and have dinner. My girlfriends provided me with all that. Did I need a man in my life? No, I don't think so, but it was an interesting two years while I tried Internet dating.

Old Ladies and Cubby Houses—2009

Karen and John didn't go out very much and had organised to attend a race day at Rosehill on a Saturday in October 2009. Mum couldn't let me have time with my grandkids while she stayed home, so she came up with me. Karen and John were all dressed up and ready to go about 1.00 p.m. As soon as they left, Mum went up the backyard with Cameron and Jade to "play" in their cubby house. Mum has never been very sensible about the agility of a woman in her late eighties, and consequently she thought it would be a good idea to walk down a ramp from the cubby to the grass. She stepped on the middle of the fold-up ramp, and it closed up around her foot, abruptly depositing her on the hard, rocky ground.

I was on the phone in the house and Cameron came running down the yard yelling and crying that Noonga, as he called her, had fallen over. I looked out the glass doors and could see her lying on the ground; I had no idea what her condition actually was. I ran up over the rocks to the top level to see what had happened. I couldn't see any blood, she was conscious and talking, and she didn't seem to have hurt her head or back. I tried to lift her up by her left arm, because she was lying on her right side, but it caused her a lot of pain. I went back down to the house, grabbed a rug and pillow, and hotfooted it back up to the top level.

I asked the kids to stay with Mum, but Cameron was almost hysterical, and all Jade wanted was her lunch. It was funny in retrospect, but not too amusing on the day. Cameron came down to the house with me and was nervously chewing the collar of his shirt because he thought it was his mistake. Apparently Mum had commented, "It will be your fault if I fall down this ramp," just before she hit the ground. Poor Cameron; he was so upset, and it wasn't his blunder at all.

I rang the ambulance and explained the situation. They arrived within about twenty minutes, and it was such a difficult job to get Mum from the top level, down over the rock steps, and through the house to the ambulance. They had to get another crew to come and help because the access was so difficult.

I rang Karen on her mobile because I didn't know what to do with the kids. She couldn't believe she and John had been gone less than twenty minutes when everything went pear-shaped. Jade was still asking when she was going to get lunch. I was trying to stop the dog from going through the house and running away up the road, consoling Cameron, answering the door to the neighbour (who had seen the ambulance and came in to see if she could help), getting Mum's medical information together so the ambulance could take it with them, and telling Jade lunch wouldn't be long. "Yes, but *how* long?" was her plaintive cry. Even with eight arms, an octopus would have had trouble coping.

The ambulance left with Mum in it, and I waited for Karen and John to come home and then went down to the hospital to see what was happening with Mum. When I arrived in the emergency department, they had her in a bed and fitted up with wires attached to monitors. After doing tests and scans, they assessed that she had a broken upper left arm, and at that stage they thought her left ankle was broken as well. Later on it was verified that it wasn't actually her ankle, but her heel that was broken. Many weeks of hospitalisation, therapy, and countless trips backwards and forwards to the hospital began. I was on first name terms with the guy on the parking area boom gate.

I felt very sorry for Cameron because he was harbouring such guilt about the accident, but gradually Karen got him to see that he had no part in what happened. It was Mum who decided to do something stupid and step on a ramp that was lying on top of stairs and half folded up. For goodness sake, she was a lady of very senior years but had never taken her age or agility into consideration when she wanted to do something "youthful".

The hospital did the best they could, but she was eighty-nine years old and bones, tissue, and tendons don't recover as well at that age. Because of a botched operation on her arm and misdiagnosis of her foot injury, she was left with a virtually useless left arm and her foot in an orthopaedic boot. I had to admire her spirit though, because she was prepared to do whatever she could to get well enough to come home. I tried to go daily to the hospital and take fresh nighties, juice, or whatever else I could do to make her stay less arduous. There was no way my mother was going to do without getting her hair done, so I took in the rollers, set her hair, and then dried it off. She was not going to be some poor little old lady sitting up in bed with messy hair. Trying to tint her hair while she was in hospital was not practical, and she certainly didn't like the idea of white roots at the base of honey blonde hair, but that was simply the way it was. I took in food that she liked, because as everyone knows hospital fare was really just to keep one alive, not send the palate to hitherto unknown heights of ecstasy. Fish and chips, quiche, homemade food, and her favourite teabags were all on the list for delivery to the hospital. As the dutiful daughter, I attended to all these things with very little in the way of thanks. The girl who brought the juice and tea trolley was appreciated more than I was; she at least came on a regular schedule, unlike me, who had to fit it in around work and replying to several phone calls a day, from Mum's answering machine, to find out how she was progressing.

By the end of seven weeks, she was recovered enough to come home—down but certainly not out. Physiotherapists visited the house, people helped shower her, and a multitude of others assisted with her medical requirements. Her other needs were to be supplied by me, whether or not I liked it, and for the most part I didn't. I was cook, dog minder, transportation, housework, receptionist, and nurse—although she did tell me that I was a lousy nurse. Sorry about that.

As is often the case with people who are sick or injured, Mum became very frustrated quite easily. I could understand this, but don't shoot the messenger. I got fed up with trying to do things and always getting them wrong—according to her, anyway. Added to this, I had her dog Bonnie to look after because she was not allowed in the house. Mum was worried that Bonnie would trip her up, so the dog moved in with me, along with scratching her fleas, tracking mud in, and trying to bite Zoe. Oh, what a joyful time that was.

I organised Mum's tablets, took her to visit her GP, set her hair, did her washing and housework, and helped her with meals—and whatever I did fell short of what she thought I should be doing. She resented it when I "escaped" for a while, as I had to do sometimes, or I would have put a pillow over her head because she pushed me so far. About the only thing that stopped me from causing her some permanent harm was that I wouldn't do jail time on her account.

As the weeks and months went by, it became obvious that she would not make a full recovery and would be unable to drive. This affected her independence, and from a purely selfish point of view, it really stuffed mine up, too. Wherever she needed to go, I would have to take her, and I wasn't looking forward to that. I felt like a mouse caught in a trap, but there was no one to release me other than myself.

For a few weeks there was a constant stream of visitors, requiring endless cups of tea and biscuits. Mum, as was her way, held court in the lounge room, and I circulated like the little maid and dispensed refreshments. I wished they would all go home so that I could go back down to my flat for a bit of peace and quiet, not to mention a wine or three—and sometimes a lot more than that.

While undergoing psychological counselling when in my fifties, I had a lot of issues about my relationship with my mother, and again they were rearing their ugly head. She was pushing my buttons, and I didn't like it. I had to find a way to disconnect myself from her never-ending criticism, so I created ways and reasons to not be there any more than I actually had to. Yes, she was my mother, but she had never shown me any respect, and I found it extremely difficult under these circumstances to want to help her any more than absolutely necessary. I didn't like her, and I don't think she liked me much, either. I had learned a very interesting phrase when going to the psychologist, and I thought it represented my feelings very accurately. I was "useful but not valuable", and that was exactly how I felt right then.

I resented having to drive her on a sixty-kilometre round trip to a club at Eastwood for her to meet up with some recently discovered people her own age. Every fortnight I would leave a space in my weekend diary, usually Sunday afternoon, so I could deliver her over to the people who had to put up with her for a few hours, and I would then dutifully return and collect her at the appointed time. I carried out her raffle prizes, got her settled in the car, and then took her home, all the way being regaled with what she considered was wrong with everyone else's life. No doubt she hadn't held back in telling them how they should be living and what they should be doing. "You need to get a life," was one of her favourite phrases, which I found rather superfluous because they were nearly all over eighty and, I was sure, had had the life they wanted by then. If not, it was already too late.

Christmas approached, and I wasn't looking forward to it. It would be another gathering of the clan, fraught with the same problems as the year before and several before that. Four generations for Christmas

Day—fabulous. In most families this would be wonderful: give people time to gather and enjoy each other's company. However, our family was not of that ilk. Having my mother, daughter, and myself in the same room was uncomfortable, especially in 2009, when I was just about at the end of my tether with her constant complaints and demands. Where had my life gone? I did have one before October 2009, but I was certainly having a hard time clawing it back, and I wasn't at all sure that I would succeed.

The first thing I decided to do early in 2010 was to change my job. I needed to get away from Mum for a few days a week, and I needed better structure in my life in terms of days worked and a stable income. I updated my resume and went to a few places to see if they had any vacancies. I found a job as a medical secretary with quite a big specialist practice, and I started my new employment at the end of January. I had been used to being the one in charge at most other places I had worked, but in this job I was just a small fish in a big pond. I didn't really want the worry and responsibility of a career; I just wanted to earn some money and have time to do other things with my life. The problem was that I didn't know what those other things were actually going to be, but I would certainly try to not be home too often and have all my "spare" days used up. I knew Mum could get help through the DVA for shopping and other errands, but she preferred me to use up my time.

Working three days a week would help me avoid my mother shouting at me from the steps at the back of her house, or coming down to the flat and flinging the door open uninvited with a demand that I do something, such as fix the remote for the TV or wash her dog. I felt that I was the home handyman on site. She constantly sat on the remote control and therefore disconnected all the programs. I had written down for her how to get the channels back on, but no, it was easier to stand on the top step and yell for me to come up and fix it. And I did, constantly. Her house had never been wired properly, so she was always tripping the safety switch. Torch in hand, I would carefully navigate my way up the side path in the dark, find something to stand on, and put the switch back on. Rarely did a word of thanks pass her ungrateful lips. I really think she thought she was entitled to her demands because that was what she had done all her life. Mum demanded, and Dad had always complied with her requests with the idea that he would get some peace, but since he'd died in 2001, she had passed the baton to me. However, I was not as amenable or as prompt to accede to her demands, and we often verbally clashed.

Drinking Alone— The World through the Bottom of a Bottle

I t is very easy to sit and consume a bottle of wine when home alone, with no one to watch me and criticise about how many drinks I was having. I was a non-drinker up until about age twenty-nine, and when I met my second husband, Jim, I didn't think he was a heavy drinker, but not a day went by that he didn't have a beer in his hand. Every night he would pour me a wine, and I continued drinking until I went to bed. On weekends the drinking for both of us often started at lunchtime on Saturday, with steak sandwiches purchased from the local pub, and it continued into the early evening; there was more drinking with dinner and so on, until we went to bed. Added to this, Jim started to make his own beer, which was cheaper and lower in alcohol, but this didn't mean he drank less of it. He gave away quite a lot and took supplies with him when he went on weekends with the army reserve. He seemed to be forever making, drinking, or disposing of an endless supply of beer. It was a good thing I was a wine drinker, or he would have had to work harder to keep up the supply.

There were many nights when I went to bed and couldn't close my eyes, because the room was spinning and I thought I would vomit. Plenty of times I was sick, but somehow I managed to get out of bed the next day and get on with whatever had to be done. For many years I didn't know what waking up after not drinking wine the night before felt like. I didn't like the feeling of being hung-over, but it was part of our lifestyle back in the seventies and until I left. I continued drinking when I was settled in the granny flat at my mother's place, but I was embarrassed about the number of bottles that I had to get rid of. I never realised how much noise two empty wine bottles made when they clanked together as I tried to sneak them past her window on my way to the bin. I even took them in the car on the way to work with me and deposited them in a roadside bin somewhere along the way.

Our recycle bin for such things as papers and bottles had a yellow lid, but I avoided that one and put the bottles in plastic bags in the red-top general rubbish bin. I knew that Mum would check my alcohol consumption if she managed to retrieve the contents of the yellow bin. It was my little guilty secret, but I could do without her finding more ammunition for criticism. In her eyes I was an alcoholic, anyway. I decided to buy four-litre wine casks to cut down on the transport noise and the cost, but I drank them way too quickly and navigated the spiral staircase a little unsteadily on several occasions. I thought that I would drink a two-litre cask a little slower, but that didn't work. The fact was that I was drinking too much, too often, and there was no one to blame but myself. I was miserable and unhappy, and I had lost my way on the path of life. I could no longer blame Jim because he wasn't there anymore to go to the fridge and get me another glass as he went past my position on the lounge, collecting my empty glass to bring me back a full one. It was too easy to consume too much in a short space of time. I never really kept track of what I was drinking because I knew I wouldn't like the tally.

My mother absolutely despised the idea of alcohol, so I took great pains to hide the evidence of my wine consumption. If I thought she was going to come down to the flat—as she often did unasked because she had no boundaries on my privacy—I didn't want her to catch me with a glass of wine in my hand at 4.30 on a Saturday afternoon. It wasn't that it had anything to do with her; it was that I didn't want to give her anything else to criticise me about. I found that if I did have a glass in my hand, I could quite easily put it on the floor and out of her sight. How pathetic—I was over sixty years old!

I was already lacking in marriage skills, as she kept reminding me, because I had been divorced twice. Yes, I knew that, because I had been involved in both divorces. I also didn't drink in front of my daughter as much as I drank at home, because she would have been horrified that I could consume a bottle plus every night.

I knew it wasn't any good for me, affected my sleep, and put on weight, but it was some sort of comfort, although I couldn't exactly explain what type. I supposed it could be along the lines of people who ate chocolate when they felt down, or mounds of hot chips. Wine was my poison of choice.

I have spoken to a lot of single friends, and many of them have gone through the same struggle. Some of my female friends have been widowed, and others divorced, but the pattern remains almost the same. First it is a scotch or wine while getting dinner, then another glass while eating dinner, followed by another drink when cleaning up. Before they realised it, half a bottle or more disappeared without them being aware of how much they had consumed. Some of these friends hadn't really drunk much while they had a partner living with them, but once on their own, drinking seemed a good idea. Some of them were ashamed of how much they drank, some said, "What the heck," and others didn't say much at all. At the bottom of all this drinking, there was pain of some sort—loneliness, disappointment, a feeling of failure, and various other triggers were apparent as I spoke to more and more women about how much they drank.

Some of these women wanted to focus on cutting down but were never specific about to what level, or even from how many each night. Others didn't care and said that it was their life, so they could do what they liked. It was apparent to me that there were a lot of women out there who were not proud of how much they drank, but it became a part of their lives. Some wanted to give it up, but a lot of them didn't because it was a comfort in some ways, a coping mechanism or a means of blotting out what they didn't like about their lives. That didn't make it right or wrong; it just made it sad on so many levels.

For myself, I had always known I shouldn't drink as much as I did, and I had made several attempts to cut down or stop. Some had been successful and others hadn't. The main problem for me was that I really didn't want to stop drinking altogether. I found it difficult to come up with a strategy such as, "I will not drink at home," and then one night after a particularly trying day, a trip down to the bottle shop on the corner destroyed that resolution. I found it easier to be the designated driver if I went out, because I would only have two drinks. However, it was not unknown for me to stop somewhere on the way home after a night out and buy a bottle of wine, just in case I felt like one or two when I get home. That was a dangerous strategy, because I knew in my heart of hearts that I would go home and probably have more than one or two.

However, I don't want to have health problems that I can prevent. I am fifteen kilograms overweight, which I need to lose. The alcohol that I consume raises my blood pressure and affects my sleep so that I am tired most mornings and don't feel like going for a walk; I'm tired all day and then start drinking again at night. It is so self-destructive, and I get really angry with myself for not having the willpower to stop drinking or even cut down to a safer level.

At my last visit to my GP, my blood pressure was the best it had been for about seven years, and I was really proud of myself. I had stopped drinking white wine and started drinking red, which I don't like as much, and therefore I consumed less. I know this sounds like a Band-Aid solution, but if I put ice cubes in the glass first and then the wine, it takes longer to drink because I am not as keen on red, and also the ice waters it down. Red wine aficionados will no doubt reel in horror, but I will give anything a go once.

I knew I needed some help with this, so in March 2012 I went back to a psychologist to try to beat this weakness as I saw it. I wanted to be more in control of how much and when I drank, but I needed to understand the why of my drinking habits. I couldn't move forward unless this made sense to me.

Fortunately I have a friend who is not much of a drinker: she will have one when she gets home, and maybe another small glass with dinner. I have asked her to be my drinking conscience, and if I head for the bottle for a third glass, she should ask me, "Do you need another one?" It might help me to not keep going after the two I have decided is enough for each night. The next move is to try to only drink a few nights a week.

I agreed with the psychologist that I need to curtail my drinking quite a lot, and cerebrally I know it is not good for me. It is thirty-five years plus of habit, and it is hard but not impossible to break. I need to learn new habits that are better for my health. Being overweight is bad for my joints, my blood pressure, and my heart; being overweight increases the possibility of diabetes. It also means I should sleep better and be more alert in the morning, which should in turn make it easier for me to go for a walk at least four mornings a week. At the end of the day, I am the only person responsible for what goes in my mouth.

The psychologist gave me a printout titled "Managing the Cravings". I was a bit taken aback because I didn't think my drinking was actually a craving, but on closer examination of what the triggers are for that first drink, it would appear that it is a longing for something that I know is really not good for my health. I have realised that I can't just have two drinks and then stop. My latest plan of attack is to only drink on Friday and Saturday nights. For the remaining five days of the week, I will try—and I stress the word *try*—to not drink. This is definitely a work in progress, but every day I don't drink is better than what my alcohol consumption used to be. I am learning the triggers for wanting to drink, such as "I have had a hard day at work, and gee, I'd love a drink." On those occasions I go to my computer, check my emails, and make a cup of tea or coffee, until the danger period of about forty-five minutes has passed.

The phrase "drowning my sorrows" is very appropriate for me. The last eight years have been tough in a lot of ways, but so rewarding in many others. I need to focus on what I have and how good my life is now, and not dwell on the past. I am drinking a lot less but still more than I should, so I consider myself a WIP (work in progress), and every day I will do the best I can; that is all I can promise at this point in time.

Evicted by My Mother—
April 2010

I n about 2006, when the people next door knocked their house down and built a larger one on the block, they asked Mum if she would like the pool filled in, and she agreed. They filled the pool up by tipping loads of clay, rock, bricks, and broken tiles down over the fence, but they also covered up all of the pebblecrete that surrounded the pool. This then allowed the weeds delivered by the birds to take over, and it was an absolute mess. The stone steps were too dangerous and unstable to take a lawnmower down there, so it was whipper-snipped every so often just to keep the weeds down. I looked out on this weed-infested demolition site from my kitchen window, and I wasn't the least bit happy. I had envisaged having a vegetable garden down there and some native shrubs to bring the birds, but that wasn't to be. Added to the difficulty of the site, the sandstone retaining wall from the top yard to the bottom level had so many hidey-holes in it for lizards and weeds that it was another area that had to be looked after. After trying over several months to get some control over the weeds, I resorted to spraying them every time I saw a green bit poking out.

In late 2009 I got back to trying to clear up this mess, and I paid for a gardener to help me. It was also somewhere I could go that Mum couldn't easily follow, and it became a sanctuary of sorts for me. We worked very hard on digging out about 1.5 metres of the dumped rock and dirt so that we could put in some new soil for the shrubs I wanted to plant. Then we had to get rid of the rest of the rubbish that was covering the pebbled edge surrounds of the pool. Next it was digging out all the weeds that had been left to multiply, putting down weed mat, and then buying more soil. It was a difficult job because there was no access to the backyard to bring loads of soil, except to come through the back of the garage. I suggested to Mum that it would make it a lot easier if we could have a load of soil delivered, but she steadfastly refused to have the back of the garage opened up, no matter what I said. Therefore, the soil had to be bought in twenty-five-litre bags from the garden centres or hardware stores, carried from the front driveway, by me, down the side of Mum's house and across the backyard, and then tipped over the rail to the bottom level. It was damned hard work, but it kept me fit. The same route had to be traversed with plants, pots, and shrubs. It was just starting to look good when she evicted me.

The day started off with a misunderstanding—nothing new between my mother and me. I had made arrangements with my daughter that I would see her when she came over on the Saturday afternoon; she said she was busy in the morning but would be over just after lunch. My mother was not privy to that particular conversation. On the basis of that time frame, I rang my male friend whom my mother had only glimpsed once or twice as he went past her window to come to my flat, and I made arrangements that we would take Zoe for a walk near the water, but I wanted to be back by lunchtime. We had a lovely time and stopped for a coffee, and I was home in plenty of time for Karen's visit that afternoon.

Soon after I arrived home, I went up to see if Mum wanted anything for lunch, and she was furious. She started off with, "You should get your priorities right."

I said, "What are you talking about?"

She was furious with me. "You should be here to see your family, not out with that dickhead."

I said, "You don't know anything about him, and what I do is none of your business."

Then she started on about how she had told me when I moved in that if I ever brought any males home, I could move out.

I was really angry about the way she spoke to me. I was not some teenager going out with the local bad boy, although I had done that in my younger years. I said to her, "I have had enough of your interfering and bad-mouthing people with whom I spend time. You have no right to tell me what to do and speak to me like you do."

She then started on about what a failure my life had been, and how I had had two marriages. She pointed out that she had had one husband and a very happy marriage. I couldn't help it—I started my own verbal attack. "You might say it was a happy marriage, but from where I observed it for forty years as an adult, it didn't look that great to me." I then told her that the reason I had had two husbands was because I married weak men, just like my father had been. Then she really lost her temper, which didn't take much for her. The rage in her face was something to behold. She was purple, her eyes glittering like two pieces of black anthracite as she raised her hand to hit me.

"If you touch me I will push you right on your arse," I warned her. As many times as my mother had hit me throughout my life, I had never hit her back or sworn at her, but now I wanted her to know that I had had enough and that there was a first time for everything.

I watched her reach down to try to pick up a pot plant from the coffee table to hit me with, and again I warned her: "Don't even think about it." I was not going to be abused any more, physically or emotionally. I had reached a stage in my life that I was taking control and would no more be a victim. She had abused me for the last time.

As I walked towards her front door, she gave me a hard push in the back, and I nearly fell through the opening. I went down to my flat and didn't know whether to cry or hit the wall with my fist in absolute frustration at this woman. She was such a nasty, vicious piece of work. I decided in those few minutes of abuse that I was going to move. I didn't care how much it cost me, but I was leaving.

I received a phone call the next morning from my mother, who lived about fifteen metres away from me, to tell me that she wanted me to leave. That suited me because it was exactly what I was going to do. The next day was a public holiday, so there was no work for me. I calculated how much money I could lay my hands on and approximately what I would need to pay a bond, rent in advance, get extra furniture, pay for getting utilities connected, and more. I knew I could do it and decided to go out the next day and look for somewhere to live. This time I hadn't prepared a running-away account, because I didn't think I was going to need it. I was wrong again.

On Tuesday I dressed nicely, did my hair and put make-up on, and set out to find a unit. I knew a real estate agent down at Ramsgate, so I set off early to find my next address. The agent told me that there wasn't anything really suitable for me in that area and advised me to try Morton, Pennington (where I used to live), and Oatville. I headed towards Morton, but I wasn't concentrating and missed the turnoff. I finished up in Oatville, the suburb where my grandparents used to live. I found a parking space and went down to get a coffee. On the way back to my car, I stopped at a real estate agent and inquired if they had any units to rent. I told them that I wanted a two-bedroom unit for myself, preferably with a garage. One of the female staff was standing in the foyer when I walked in, and she mentioned a unit to the young guy behind the desk. The unit hadn't even been put on the market because they had only taken the photos on the weekend, and the first viewing wasn't until the next day. I asked them if I could have a look at it that day because I had to work on the Wednesday. They rang the owner and arranged for me to go and see it within the next half hour. I took two steps inside the door and said, "Yes, this is what I want. Where do I sign?" I walked back down to the agent's office and arranged that I would send financial statements and whatever other paperwork they wanted that same afternoon. I got a phone call at 5.15 p.m. to tell me that I had been successful in renting the unit, and I could take possession in just under four weeks. I was so happy that I had managed to find something really nice in which to live. I didn't have a lot of furniture, but I had enough.

The only downside was that I couldn't take my dog with me into a unit, and I couldn't afford to rent a house. I would have to get her rehoused. I was very sad about that but had to be realistic and knew I would be able to find her a good home. There were plenty of people who I thought would take her for me, but I was determined I wasn't going to take her to the RSPCA with the risk of her being euthanised. She had been too good a little mate for that to happen to her.

Many people kindly offered to take her, but my daughter said she could come and live at their place, and I was very grateful for that because I had had her for nine years. She was a lovely little dog, didn't bark and was generally quiet, was small, and didn't cost much to feed—the perfect pet. I was also very glad that she was close enough that I could see her and take her for walks; she wasn't completely lost to me.

I didn't see my mother until Saturday, when she came down to the flat and flung the door open without knocking, as she usually did. She came in, sat herself down on the lounge, and announced, "I think this has gone on long enough," which meant that she has had enough of being ignored and having to fend for herself.

I said, "Well, it won't be going on much longer, because I am moving."

That got her attention and she asked, "Where are you going?"

I replied, "I am moving into a unit in Oatville."

She suddenly realised that unit and dog don't usually go together, and with a smirk on her face she asked me, "And what are you going to do with Zoe?"

I was getting quite teary by then and told her, "I will have to get her rehoused."

She looked absolutely delighted but couldn't help saying, "That's just typical of you. You only ever worry about yourself." She turned to her dog, held Bonnie's face in her hands, and said, "I wouldn't do that to you, darling."

I had had enough. I stood up and said, "Yes, but I don't kick my dog." I walked across to the door and held it open. "I didn't invite you down here, so please leave." She got up and left the flat. I didn't think that conversation worked out quite the way she had planned.

I went to work on Wednesday and then started packing on Thursday. It was going to be a big job, because I had to clean out under her kitchen as well where all my craft materials were stored, and they were on shelves, not packed in boxes. I knew that if I left anything behind, it would be thrown out.

I didn't speak to her for the next three weeks, mainly because I didn't want to but also because I didn't actually see her. I knew she wouldn't be too pleased about me packing stuff up in the garage, and the roof leaked anyway, so it was not a good place to store furniture or boxes that were uncovered. I lived in amongst the cardboard box towers for about two weeks until my son-in-law intervened and said that we would be putting stuff in the garage and "That would be all right, wouldn't it?" My mother thought the sun, moon, and stars shone out of John, so of course she agreed.

Fortunately we were having a council clean-up on the weekend before I was due to move, so things were discarded—not necessarily things I wanted to get rid of, but I knew that I couldn't take everything with me. It must have been "quality junk" because there wasn't much left when the Council truck came on the Monday to collect it. I would have preferred to have a garage sale, mainly for the money I could have raised, but that was not possible given that my mother wasn't speaking to me, and it was her garage that I would have had to use.

I packed about fifty boxes with clothes, household goods, linen, and my hobby supplies. By Friday, 21 May 2010, I was ready to go. John had organised for a truck with a lift on the back, and we went to pick it up midday. He drove it over to my mother's place, and I helped him pack it until Karen and the kids came over after school. Cameron had a great time raising and lowering the tailgate with the remote while John, Karen, and I hefted the furniture and boxes into the back.

By 7.30 that night the truck was packed, the flat was empty, and Karen and I had cleaned it. Mum was standing on the front veranda watching us pack the truck, and I asked her, "Are you happy now?"

All she said was, "I want the garage remote back." I threw it across the grass, and it landed at her feet.

My daughter was really angry at both of us for the way we were behaving, but I didn't think she realised how hurt I was at being evicted at age sixty-five just because I had a strictly platonic relationship with a male friend. The whole thing was ridiculous. It had also cost me thirty thousand dollars to have the flat renovated, and I wasn't likely to get any of that back anytime soon.

We parked the truck up at Karen's place and left again at 7.00 on Saturday morning. I was still on good terms with Jim and asked him if he could help John carry the heavier things up the thirty-four steps to my new abode. He was willing to give a hand and was rewarded with some casseroles to store in his freezer. I was very grateful for his assistance because I don't know how much help Karen and I would have been in getting the refrigerator, washing machine, dryer, and the lounge up the stairs. By 9.30 a.m., the truck was emptied, and John was on his way back to the hire depot. I couldn't believe the speed that all this stuff was brought up the three flights of stairs.

My daughter, son-in-law, and the two children were amazing. Boxes were unpacked, and the kids (aged eight and five) carried the empty cartons downstairs and stacked them in piles in the garage, ready to be tied together. Cupboards were filled, china and glass were unpacked, and even the bed was made before 5.00 that afternoon. Were we tired? Hell, yes! But I was installed in my new home, and my dog also had a new place to live. Perhaps now I would get a bit of peace.

Kate Moving In

I met Kate when she came to work as a temp in February 2010, and we had an instant rapport. We were both Sagittarians and had a lot of similarities, but we were different in many ways, too. For the six weeks we worked together, we got to know each other quite well. She was leaving for Melbourne at the end of March, and we wanted to stay in touch. I was only too well aware that when people worked together and then circumstances separated them, the friendship often failed, but in our case it went on to bigger and better things.

I had never lived in a unit before and found that although I felt safe on the third floor, I rarely saw anyone and felt quite isolated at times. One weekend I didn't speak to anyone face-to-face from the time I left work on Friday afternoon until I walked back into the office on Monday morning. I missed my dog Zoe so much that I bought a battery-operated breathing dog, Barnaby, who came complete with his own little bed. I used to put him on the lounge beside me and stroke his real-feeling fur. I was very lonely, and it was the first time in my life I hadn't had an animal living with me.

I went to Melbourne in July 2010 to see Kate, and we had a wonderful time exploring the city even though the weather was not all that great. We stayed in touch until she could come to Sydney in December, by which time we had started talking about her sharing my unit when she came up here to live, which was planned for early in 2011. It was important to be honest about our individual expectations. This was no time to have a hidden agenda if our domestic situation was to be a success.

During her December visit to Sydney, I mentioned to Kate that I really missed having pets around me, but the Strata laws of the unit block expressly forbade any animals. This was because the woman across the landing from me had a yappy white dog that had driven everyone mad for years. However, I am not always compliant when I am told I can't do something. With Kate's encouragement (and I must admit I didn't need much of that), we went out on the Saturday afternoon with the express purpose of getting a cat. I didn't want a young kitten but a more mature female, just like us. We called into a pet shop on the way to the animal shelter and bought a carry cage and some bedding. On arrival at the animal shelter, we asked about buying an older cat and were shown into a room with cages where we could take a cat out and see what her temperament was like. We worked our way around the room, and in the corner we saw this young female who wasn't feeling too good because she had just had her baby department removed. She was a tabby, which I liked, and she seemed fairly quiet. Her name was Chloe. More important, she had been an indoor animal and wasn't craving the great outdoors, which she wouldn't be getting if I took her home. She had been surrendered because her previous owner had a demented boyfriend who had threatened to put the cat in the washing machine, dryer, or microwave. I took her out of the cage, and Chloe and I fell in love.

On the journey home in the car, Chloe made her displeasure quite plain at being transported in a cage to some unknown destination. It then occurred to us that carrying a cat in a cage upstairs, in a unit block that was supposed to be animal free, was a bit of a giveaway. We decided to take our chances and got up the stairs as quickly as possible. We were in luck: nobody was around. We installed Chloe in her new home with some toys and a lovely padded bed, which we put under a chair by the windows.

Chloe still hates cages and when I have had to take her out of the unit on inspection days by the real estate agents, or for her yearly needles, she is one very annoyed tabby. She won't "talk" to either of us when she comes home and turns her back. Actions speak louder than words.

Paying for Chloe was probably one of the best investments I have every made. She is a wonderful companion when Kate is not home, and she fits in very well to our all-female household. The humans don't run the show here; our furry feline is very much in charge. She spends the morning in Kate's room, usually on the windowsill, and then has an afternoon sun bake on the carpet in my room. At night she is allowed out onto the plant-filled balcony to hunt the bugs and moths that are attracted to the light from the lounge room. I wouldn't mind having her life!

I called into my daughter's place with Kate on the way to the airport, and Karen took an instant dislike to her. I had no idea why, and I didn't really care, because this was my life, and I couldn't see any difficulties with sharing a unit with Kate. It would help both of us financially, and neither of us wanted to live alone. I had already tried it, and given the choice, I would rather avoid that lonely existence.

When Kate returned to Melbourne, I started to make space in the unit for her anticipated arrival sometime in March. I had never been a really tidy person, and I knew that Kate was, so it was up to me to lift my housekeeping standards. I knew that Kate would be a good influence on me because she ate well, exercised, and only drank a little. All of these things could be improved on in my life, and because she was a better housekeeper, I would have a tidier place in which to live. What more could a girl want?

My daughter made it clear to me that she wouldn't be coming over once Kate moved in, and I was very disappointed about that. I knew she didn't like Kate, but this was my life, and I wished Karen would let me get on with it. If it didn't work out with Kate, then I would move onto plan B, whatever that was.

I had moved into the largest bedroom when I first came to live in the unit. I decided to stay in that room because it meant that I could put the fold-down lounge in there with my single bed, and if my grandchildren came over, they could stay in my room. I was very upset when my daughter informed me they would not be coming to stay once Kate moved in. I couldn't get any explanation from her and knew I wouldn't be able to persuade Cameron and Jade to have a sleepover with me. This was on top of Karen informing me that she wouldn't be calling in for a cuppa, either. It was very hurtful and felt like another round of punishment, but if they didn't want to come over to see me, then that was their decision.

I felt that I was being reprimanded for walking out on my mother, and therefore in Karen's mind I had left her with that responsibility. It was up to her if she wanted to take up that duty, but from my point of view I didn't expect her to do that. Mum was at least 50 per cent to blame for me moving out of Beresford, but I felt that Karen didn't see it that way.

I spent many hours transporting bits and pieces down to the garage so that Kate would have a room of her own when she arrived in Sydney. I had certainly spread myself around the unit, and it was time to consolidate the furniture. I put up extra shelving in the garage and somehow made all the excess stuff fit in there, with room for the car.

I had only just finished making space in drawers, cupboards, and shelves when Kate was due to arrive. On 22 March 2011, she finally made it to Sydney, and I had made up a sign that said, "Welcome to Your New Home—Janet and Chloe." I was surprised that most of her worldly possessions were contained within a very small car. I was more than happy that she didn't have a removalist van full of furniture, or I wouldn't have known where to put it all. I certainly couldn't store it at Karen's place.

As soon as Kate arrived, there was a great feeling of friendship in the house. We were on the same wavelength, and there was an air of optimism that all would be well in the future. We had agreed on several occasions that if something wasn't working for either of us, we would say so—nicely.

Kate slept on the lounge in my room for a few days, and we needed to go shopping for her bedroom furniture. IKEA was the obvious choice for several reasons: first, the price of the furniture, and second, the fact it was flat-packed and could be manoeuvred up three flights of stairs. Well, that was the theory.

With credit card in one hand and a list in the other, we headed for IKEA. What an adventure that turned out to be. We were IKEA virgins and didn't know the drill for choosing furniture, marking down the aisle and bay number it was in, and then loading it onto a trolley. We thought that it was sufficient to record the item number, and someone at the checkout would go to the racks and retrieved it for us. Not so! By the time we discovered that we had to actually get the queen-size bed, wardrobes, bedside tables, chest of drawers, and mattress out of the racks ourselves, we already had a trolley full of pillows, sheets, doona cover, and a multitude of other bits and pieces to go towards making our house a home.

Reality check! Our trolley was full, and it was taking two of us to actually push it towards the checkout. Then we were faced with how we were going to extract Kate's bedroom furniture from the racks and transport it to the checkout when we were already loaded up to the hilt. We managed to find an IKEA man, who probably needed a stiff drink after we had finished with him, and he kindly got a flat trolley and started to load it up. We couldn't see around it, or over it, and with two of us pushing two trolleys, we were more than a danger to shins and ankles if someone stopped in front of us.

Not to be daunted and with a mission to accomplish, we pushed and shoved all these household goodies to the checkout area and sailed through a wide, open space as we thought that because it was home delivery, we should proceed straight to the clearly labelled "Home Delivery Help Desk". Again we were mistaken. We were sternly told by an IKEA man in a yellow shirt that we hadn't paid for the goods. Well, we knew that and were heading for the home delivery desk to take care of the bill. We then had to turn the flatbed trolley around with all the bedroom stuff on it, followed by the shopping trolley full to the brim, in a space that was about the size of a small car. Well, if ever anything was going to put one's back out, it was this manoeuvre. However, being strong of mind but maybe not so much in body, we managed it with a lot of pushing and shoving interspersed with a few four-letter words. We made our way back through the crowd of customers who were queued up to pay for their goods before trying to make a run for the home delivery desk. They had probably been there before and knew the drill—hence the smug smiles on their faces.

We managed to find a space at the end of a reasonably short line, and it wasn't long before we found out why others had abandoned this particular queue. The lady who was at the front and purchasing some goods had a credit card that wouldn't accept the sale. I seemed to have a talent for getting on the wrong line, and once again I had achieved just that. Oblivious to those behind her, mainly us, she proceeded to ring her husband on her mobile and got no joy there.

She rang the bank and got the same response, so she then set about removing the number of goods it would require to bring the bill down to the amount she could afford to pay. Naturally she required some of the space we were occupying, and by now other shoppers were lining up behind us. It then required me to go to the back of the queue and ask those people if they would move back about a metre and so on down the line to the front. I felt like they thought I was the idiot because I had forgotten to do something, and by that time I was at the end of my tether and couldn't be bothered explaining that it was the woman at the front who had to unpack half of her trolley because her credit card wouldn't accept the charge, and we needed the space to back up so that she had room for the rejects.

After paying for our goods, we were allowed to proceed to the home delivery area to arrange for transport of all the furniture on the flatbed. Our enthusiasm for setting up home with all the other goodies we had bought deluded us into taking them with us. That part was all right because we got them in the car, but only just. It was an exercise in space minimisation and management on how to get everything in without bits sticking out the windows or getting caught in the door. A glass of wine would have gone well right about then, but I was driving home, so no go!

Of course it was when we got home we realised the error of our decision. There were three flights of stairs to carry all this stuff up; we could have had it all delivered the next day. What a pair of dummies! We did have that wine when we got home and, surrounded by the contents of the car, started to unpack and unwrap all the bits and pieces. Luckily it was garbage night, so it was up and down the stairs again with all the packaging. I was exhausted when it was time to go to bed, but we had achieved such a lot in one day, and tomorrow the furniture was due to arrive.

I had put flat-pack furniture together before and didn't think I would have much of a problem. However, my enthusiasm was right out of kilter with my actual skills and just unpacking the stuff was a challenge. What masochist designed this packaging? We had mountains of cardboard, plastic wrapping tape, and polystyrene foam in many weird shapes all over the lounge room, with nowhere to actually assemble the furniture. After more trips down to the recycle bins at the side of the units, eventually we had managed to get rid of the cardboard out of the living area, to give us some working space.

Kate admitted that she was not very handy with screwdrivers and tools, so we made a deal that I would put the furniture together and she would clean up the front balcony. That seemed fair to both of us. Kate got her rubber gloves ready, a bucket of hot soapy water, and a scrubbing brush before she headed outside. I don't think either of us realised just how many birds had pooped on the walls and floor over the past year, when I had encouraged them to feed there by leaving out seed and fruit. I treated them as though they were extra pets, and sometimes there were up to twenty birds clustered around the feed tray. What went in one end must come out the other, and birds seemed to have a very fast digestive system—and it came in a range of colours, from cream to dark brown. It was all a very decorative feature of the stone top on the brick balcony and dripped very artistically down the cream-painted wall on the inside. Pools of it also abounded on the white tiles and looked less than attractive.

We needed this furniture put together because we couldn't get to the bathroom without holding the queen-size mattress away from the wall and stepping around several parts of a bedroom suite. Added to this, I had tried to put a three-seater lounge together and had succeeded up to the point when one of the arms fell off. I didn't know a lot, but I knew when I was beaten, and this was one of those times.

With great optimism, Kate and I agreed it would only take a few hours to put the furniture together, but with ignorance came bliss. After one and a half hours and only one small bedside table partly constructed (mainly because I had to take the back off and reverse it), and a lounge with an arm hanging off, I decided to call in someone with knowledge of assembly: my brother. Charlie had been trained as a cabinetmaker with an antique reproduction company, and the idea of flat pack offended his fine detail skills, but he agreed to come down and help me. I told him to bring a power screwdriver because my wrist was all screwed out.

He duly arrived about forty-five minutes later, complete with toolkit, and looked at our living area with a mixture of disgust and dismay. It was a bit of a mess, but I had at least gotten rid of the cardboard and kept all the bits for each piece of furniture together, so that was something good, I supposed.

In the meantime, Kate had been scrubbing and rubbing the walls and floor of the outdoor space for what seemed like hours to her, in order to remove all traces left by my feathered friends. My regular lorikeets were a bit confused when they came for their seed and fruit breakfast the next morning, and they found a pristine space with no signs of food. The sulphur-crested cockatoos were a bit more persistent, and when they landed on the stone top of the balcony wall, Kate squirted them with a spray bottle filled with water. After a few days they got the message and found somewhere else to dine. With Kate's hard work, we now had a lovely outdoor room, with a table for two and comfy cane chairs, plants that would flourish, and a pleasant place to sit and have dinner in the warmer weather.

Lunch, several cups of tea, and dinner followed before Kate's bedroom furniture was assembled. I think our estimation of a couple of hours was rather ambitious, not to mention naive. Good thing we weren't doing this for a living, or we would be on bread and water. As my very tired brother packed up his toolkit, ready to leave, he told me, "Sis, if you ever buy flat-pack furniture again, lose my number." I wasn't brave enough to tell him then that we still needed some stuff from IKEA, but after my brother's departing statement, Kate decided to ask her unsuspecting nephew to help assemble her latest acquisition of a desk. We fed him, but funnily enough after three hours of battling with the desk instructions, he also mentioned that he would be quite pleased if we never called him again for furniture construction. We were fast running out of assemblers!

Finishing touches such as lamps and cushions were added over the next few months, and we hung pictures. I put a favourite picture up behind my bed but didn't realise that because of the weight of the frame and glass, those removable "tenant friendly", stick-on hooks wouldn't hold it for long. Fortunately I was in the lounge room when it came crashing down between the wall and the back of my bed, smashing all the glass and denting the frame. I think I would have died of fright if I had been in bed when the picture made its descent.

Unfortunately, not everyone liked my choices of the change I had made to my life. Some friends and family didn't approve, but it was my life, and it was nice to have someone to go and have a coffee with, share a meal, and help with the expenses. "Walk a mile in what were my lonely shoes, and see if you would like that life," was generally my response to any criticism.

Dad's oft-repeated mantra was, "Anything for peace sake." He didn't realise, even up until his death, that you don't get peace with a bully unless you stand up to them. No man has ever stood up for me, including my father, brother, and both husbands. Mum was always putting me down for being married twice, and she tried to tell me that Dad was the love of her life. Give me a break! I was an adult for at least forty of the years they were married, and if that was a successful marriage, then I will eat Dad's old fishing hat.

It has only been since my grandchildren have been at school that I understood I had been bullied by my mother for most of my adult life. When I finally stood up for myself and told her a few home truths, I had to find somewhere else to live. Telling me to leave where I had been living for six years was the only power she had over me. My parting words to her were, "Be careful what you wish for."

I have what I call my Grateful Book, and in that I record, as often as I can, all the wonderful things in my life. I have a job, a roof over my head, food in the cupboard, and a bit of money in the bank. On a personal level, I have a great daughter and son-in-law, and two wonderful grandchildren, all of whom I love dearly. I have friends who have stood by me through thick and thin, and when the going got rough, they stuck around.

Family and friends have commented that they see me as a strong person with a "Don't mess with me" attitude, but this is because I have always had to rely on myself to survive, and I think I have done a pretty good job so far.

Zoe: 10.8.2001 to 20.10.2012

I remember seeing Zoe as a little puppy in the pet shop at Westfield jumping up at the side of the cage and wanting me to take her home. I had actually gone to see the movie *Pearl Harbour* with my mother, and as usual we were ridiculously early for the film, so we decided to have a look around the centre. As always, I was drawn to the pet shop because that's the way I was. To me, animals were far more honest and loving than most humans, and their love was unconditional. I had always had pets but they were family animals, not one chosen by me and just for me. Jim had said no more pets, but I took no notice of him. He didn't feed or bathe them, do the trips to the vet, or clean up after them, so I didn't think he could make that call.

Zoe was the cutest little black and white dog with a very pretty face. She was supposed to be a miniature fox terrier, but I think her mother might have been a bit friendly with the whippet or Italian greyhound up the road, because Zoe could run like the wind—usually away from me.

We had a pool in the backyard with a security fence around it of upright metal posts spaced about fifteen centimetres apart. This would have kept most dogs behind it, but not Zoe. She could put one of her long, skinny front legs through between the bars, twist her body, and then put her head through, and voila she was out. She was smart enough to come up the back steps onto the veranda of the house. It wasn't that she wanted to run away; she just wanted to be with her people—namely me. As soon as I let her in the back door, she headed for the lounge and settled herself down with a very satisfied sigh. Mission accomplished, and Zoe won again.

I would have to have been the worst trainer possible to have a dog like Zoe. I let her do whatever made her happy. If she wanted to sit on the lounge, I made space for her. When I called her and she didn't come to me, I chased after her but never caught her; she would come back when she felt like it. These were all very bad traits in me that I couldn't control a little dog, but I loved her so.

She was born to run. My friends Maryanne and James had a poodle named Ginger who was great mates with Zoe. He would even let her eat out of his bowl, but he wouldn't let any other dog do that. We had many happy outings over eleven years with these two dogs running and playing just like the puppies they were in their heads, if not their bodies. Ginger ran and Zoe chased him, circled him, and beat him back to where we were standing. Ginger chased the ball, and Zoe chased him but was never interested in toys of her own. Ginger loved the water and would take a flying leap into whatever water he could find, clean or dirty, whereas Zoe came to a screeching halt at the water's edge. A bath was okay, but that other water with no edges was not a favourite place for her.

In September and October, Zoe began to deteriorate. It started with a cough, and the vet established that she had a heart murmur of between grade three and four, though she didn't need to be on medication yet. She was losing her usual get-up-and-go, wasn't all that interested in food, and was starting to lose weight. I put most of this down to her age, at eleven, but I could see she was also becoming very lethargic. She no longer imitated a jumping pogo stick and spent more time lying down, which concerned me.

When I went to Maryanne's the last few times when Zoe was sick, Ginger heard my car and came out looking for her. After he had established that she wasn't with me, he didn't want to have anything to do with me; I was simply the transport for his little mate.

My daughter rang me one wet night in September and asked me to come up and have a look at Zoe, because the dog seemed to be having trouble breathing. I was shocked when I saw her and knew she needed veterinary care. My granddaughter Jade had been caring for my dog for almost three years after I had been evicted from the granny flat behind my mother's house. Zoe and their Jack Russell terrier, Sam, got on well, and there hadn't been any problems. Jade loved Zoe and carried her around draped across her little arms, with Zoe's long legs hanging down. Jade was only five years old when Zoe went to live there, but not once did she drop Zoe, and she was so loving with her.

I rang the emergency vet at the St George Animal Hospital, and they would see her. It was 8.30 p.m., and Jade wanted to come with me, so off we went out into the wind and rain. Jade didn't want to go to bed until she found out what was wrong with Zoe, so she came to the vet in her pyjamas and dressing gown. I was surprised my daughter let her come with me because it was Jade's bedtime, but I was glad of her company.

The vet had a quick look at Zoe and admitted her so she could have oxygen to help with her breathing. I could see her chest and ribs heaving with the effort to get some air into her fluid-filled lungs. Jade answered all the questions about how much she ate and drank, and we left Zoe behind. I was asked to ring the next morning to see how she was going. She had improved overnight but certainly wasn't her old self. She only weighed 5.8 kilograms, so she had lost 1.2 kilograms in about a month.

She was only home with Jade a few days before she deteriorated again. I took her back to the vet, they admitted her for treatment, and I picked her up that afternoon. She looked a bit brighter and wasn't struggling so much for breath. Her medication was increased, but unfortunately after two days she went downhill again. I had her to the vet three times in ten days, and it was established that she had congestive heart failure that no medication could reverse. This meant that because her heart wasn't working properly, her kidneys would shut down and lead to a very painful death.

On Friday night, 19 October 2012, I again got a call from Karen that Zoe was struggling. I had had a wine or two, so I took a taxi up to my daughter's place. I could see Zoe wasn't at all well. Her chest was heaving with the effort of trying to breathe. I decided to take her home with me and monitor her throughout the night. My cat Chloe had never been up close and personal with a dog before, and she wasn't sure what to make of this thing that had arrived in her domain. Zoe was really quiet and sat on my lap, but she couldn't sleep. Her breathing was laboured, and she kept doing an awful cough, trying to clear her lungs. I knew she was getting near the end of her life, so I dropped down the lounge bed in my room, and the two of us slept together. How I had missed her doing this. She had slept on my bed for eight years before she went to live at my daughter's place. I kept waking up to see if she was still with us, and by morning I was exhausted mainly from lack of sleep, but also because I was dreading what the day would bring.

Saturday morning, 20 October 2012, I took her to the vet, and Jade came with me. Jade and I had already had conversations about dogs "getting a needle", and she understood why this had to be done in some cases. There was nothing more they could do to help Zoe, and I couldn't keep her alive for my sake and let her go through renal failure before death. The vet and I explained this to Jade, and although she was very upset, she understood that this was what was best for Zoe. We took Zoe home and gave Jade a few hours with her so that she could say her good-byes. It was so sad watching her cuddle Zoe for the last time, whispering into her ear, and dashing away her tears with her spare hand. A friend of Jade's had just been through a similar thing with their dog, so she understood about euthanasia and why it had to be done, but she was only eight years old and loved this little dog so much.

When I was at the vet on the Saturday morning, he gave me a brochure on different ways the pet's ashes could be kept. Jade chose a Keepsake Eddy bear and wrote a little verse to be embroidered onto the bear's foot: "I love you and you love me, and together we will always be." What a bizarre way to spend a Saturday morning, with Karen, Jade, and me sitting on the lounge choosing from a Petrest brochure to keep some of Zoe's ashes. If this would help to ease Jade's grief, then I was all for it. I chose a small stone containing ashes that I could take with me wherever I went. It now resides in its own special place beside my bed.

Karen asked Jade if she could take some photos of her with Zoe, but Jade didn't want Karen to take photos of her crying. Most of the photos were the back of Jade's head with Zoe's face hard up against it as she cuddled her.

I told Jade that I had to take Zoe at 2.30, and it was so hard watching her face, tears running down her cheeks as she said good-bye to her little friend. Jade gave me a small, fluffy dog that she had bought for Zoe that morning to send with her to the crematorium, and it was at that point that I almost lost it completely.

Cameron couldn't bring himself to say good-bye to Zoe, and that was okay, too. We all react in our own way, and it doesn't mean that some feel the grief more or less based on the tears shed. Karen was struggling not to cry for Jade's sake. I had sunglasses on, and we finally had to leave. I gave Jade Zoe's collar and tag for a keepsake, which she put on display in the lounge room. The three of us went down to the car, and I put Zoe on the front seat, with the little fluffy toy Jade had given her. It was so hard trying to get the door closed so I could leave. I could hardly see to drive because the tears were running down my face, but if I didn't go then, I didn't think I could make it to the vet.

When I got there, they took me straight in, explained what they were going to do, and checked again with me that it was what I wanted. I held her little face between my hands and watched the light go from her eyes. She was so trusting, so loving for the eleven years she lived.

Zoe's death closed a chapter of my life filled with all sorts of joy and sadness. In her short lifetime my grandson and granddaughter were born, and I had left my husband, changed jobs several times, and changed addresses. Here I was at the end of 2012 living in a rented unit with a very bossy cat (which I was not supposed to have). Even Barnaby, the battery-operated dog I'd bought in July 2010 because I was so lonely without my Zoe, was not much comfort.

When Jade told my mother that Zoe had died, Mum asked why Jade was so upset because it hadn't been her dog. This really upset Jade because to her, Zoe was her dog and she missed her terribly.

For my birthday in November, Karen had an enlarged black-and-white photo of Jade and Zoe framed. She could not have chosen a better gift.

My Friends Are like Gold

As we go through life, we meet so many people. Some stay with us for quite a long time, and others pass through with only a minimal impact on our life while their journeys with us last.

To have a really good friend is gold. They are the ones who will stand by you no matter what you do, the ones who are instinctively there for you when life is dealing you a lousy hand. They don't judge; they simply support and listen, sometimes offering an opinion, but mostly they want to help you for no gain on their part.

I have friends who have been part of my life for over thirty years, yet they are entirely dissimilar from each other. They are different in personality and the way they go about solving life's problems. They have each come into my life separately, one when my daughter was only five years old and another almost ten years later. Other women I have met through work and our friendships have been of a much shorter duration, but all it takes is a phone call, and we are always there for each other.

There are other friends who are just as staunch and will listen, just as I will listen to them when they want to unload. Sometimes that is all it takes—to be able to unburden to someone who won't start telling you where you are going wrong and what you should do, unless asked to do so.

At times silence and a box of tissues work better with a cup of tea, and on other occasions only a glass of wine will suffice. The important thing is to be there when your friends are not having a good day. There may be nothing concrete you can do, but you can listen. That doesn't mean umm-ing and aah-ing in all the right spots; it means *really* listening to the raw pain in a friend's voice, watching the tears drip down her cheeks and off the end of her nose before she realises that she is actually crying. A hug around shoulders that are shaking with emotion doesn't go astray either, but it has to be genuine. Not just a hug with the inference, "Well, you're all right now, so I'll go and get my bus," but more along the lines of, "I know you're not all right yet, and I will stay with you until you no longer need me, however long that takes."

Sometimes friends may be blind to their partner's or children's faults, but if you are truly a friend, you won't shine a spotlight on that particular issue. Most people know their nearest and dearest aren't perfect, but it is no help to have that pointed out when they are in pain from something that has happened. Leave that one alone, because in your own world, does it make a difference to you if someone criticises your close ones? Of course it does, and there are times when you can wear it and other times when it just makes you angry—not with the person who is causing the pain, but with your friend who has pointed out the shortcomings. This is a lose-lose situation.

A mother, wife, sister, or child can say awful things about a relative, but if anyone else voices the same opinion, she will go for the jugular. There are boundaries within a friendship that must never be crossed, if the friendship is to go on to bigger and better things and survive. It is of absolutely no assistance whatsoever if the person you are trying to help feels that you are betraying her by bringing up previous misdeeds by her loved one, although at the moment she could probably strangle that person herself.

A good, solid friendship doesn't need to be conducted in beautiful and rich surroundings. It can be as simple as sharing some time with a cup of coffee simply for the pleasure of being together, having a few laughs and catching up on what has been happening in each other's lives. However, the balance of a good friendship can be delicate at times; those involved in the friendship need to know when to speak and when to only nod. There has to be an exchange of ideas, not one person lecturing the other with all that has been happening in his or her life. This is too lopsided, and one of the participants will come away from that get-together feeling that she has been verbally battered and hasn't been able to talk about what is real for her. This will alter the chemistry for the next time they get together, and it may disintegrate from a great friendship to a thought process of, "Why bother? I never get a word in, anyway."

If you put all my friends in one room, they would probably have very little in common with each other. Some I go with to movies, plays, or theatre; others I enjoy a simple lunch somewhere that is not financially challenging, and I walk my dog with others. I like to go on holidays with a few of them, but wouldn't dream of even asking others because it was not their thing. I had a wonderful holiday in Italy with a girl I was working with, and we have remained friends ever since.

I am conscious of keeping in touch with my friends, preferably in person, but the next best thing is by telephone. I resist doing the e-mail thing because to me, it is much better to hear a person's voice than to read what someone is doing. By hearing my friends, I can better judge how life is treating them, and they can do the same for me. A text message is all that is required to make arrangements, but if I haven't been able to catch up in person, I like to talk with them a bit longer.

When I left my husband, my genuine friends kept me afloat and did what they could so that I didn't fall into the depths of depression. They helped me with practical things such as packing and unpacking my worldly goods, or going out for an impromptu meal simply because they sensed I needed company. I will be eternally grateful for all of this.

Family cannot replace the value of a good friend, no matter how well meaning they are. They are basically coming from a different place and are often not privy to secrets I would tell a friend. One of my friends knows more about me than any other person on this earth, simply because we have a trust that goes back a long way. We don't always agree, but we disagree with respect.

The variety of my friends' personalities' likes and dislikes provides me with a rich tapestry of people whose company I enjoy, and I like to think that it is reciprocal. They were always there for me when things got tough, and at times I lost my way, but as the saying goes, what doesn't kill you makes you stronger, so thank you to all the wonderful women in my life. I couldn't have done it without you.

My daughter wrote this poem for me in 2000, and I think it beautifully sums up how I feel about the importance of friendship.

The Friendship of Flowers

A true friendship is like a flower:
It starts off with a seed.
The seed can grow with love and trust,
Or demise into a weed.

The friendship blossoms as a flower will grow,
And some nutrients are required.
Being honest, love, and companionship,
And to each other feel admired.

Throughout time, the flower may wilt,
And if not looked after may die.
As a friendship may come across obstacles,
And you have to wonder why.

But as the flower is given more water,
The strength of it will return
As the flame of a true friendship
Will still continue to burn.

If we can achieve but one thing in life,
Before it will come to an end,
It's a proud thing to be able to say
That you are someone's best friend!

Off the Scale

I have never really thought much about how old I am. The years come and go celebrated by a birthday, but other than that sometimes I feel as though I am in my forties, and on other days it seems that a century is just around the corner. It has been brought home to me lately by the media that my age makes me ineligible for so many things. Let me explain. As I go through a well-known women's magazine, I see advertisements for clothing suitable for women in their twenties, thirties, forties, fifties . . . and then nothing. Does that mean I should go around naked? I wouldn't think so, but obviously it is not worth their while sourcing out clothing to try to make a sixty-plus woman be suitably dressed for public view.

Is that the fault of the manufacturers, or is it that the magazine has no more space to devote to the second half of the century people?

Those same people, who have time to shop, are cashed up and want to look smart, but media and retailers alike mostly ignore them.

And as I turn over the pages, the previous scenario is the same with make-up. A twenty-something girl is advertising "age-defying mousse" with not a line on her airbrushed face. What would she know about age defying, or is the mousse so good that she is actually fifty-five? I have used "age defying" make-up, but I think I should have started a little earlier.

There are articles on cream for hands, but none of those hands show the dreaded brown age spots. The only place you find those ads is in the seniors papers or on some pyramid of tubes in the chemist with dreadful before-and-after photos propping them up. Yuck! No arthritic knuckles are seen anywhere in the pages of the women's magazines, and in this day and age you don't have to be old to have bumpy fingers. I will agree that it would be almost impossible to get before-and-after photos of hands deformed by arthritis and then miraculously brought back to pristine state, but that doesn't mean we of the bumpy group don't want the skin on our hands to look nice.

The same applies to our nails. Just because our nail bed starts just a bit above a lumpy knuckle doesn't mean we don't desire Siren Red nail polish. There is still a bit of a vamp in us somewhere; we just have to look harder.

Even funeral insurance is denied to some of us once we make it to sixty-five. Does that mean they think we are not going to live long enough for our premiums of "just seventy cents a day" to reach the ten thousand dollars deemed to be the present cost of a funeral?

Probably, but why not just charge us more? Oh well, it looks as though my daughter will have to cover the cost of my send-off because I haven't been able to join up and pay seventy cents a day.

It must be assumed that those of us who are still working are rich, because we can't access work insurance, either. As there is no legal retirement age, and many of us work because we don't have a huge amount of money behind us, why is it that we can't get insurance that will pay us if we are unable to work due to sickness or accident? It is the young who need insurance because they play sports on the weekend and break and twist bits of their bodies. The young are also the people up on unsteady ladders, renovating their homes and falling to the ground, spending weeks off work. It is the young who drive their cars too fast and have accidents, as proven by many statistics, not the seniors. Therefore, I think the insurance companies are throwing their money at the wrong market. It is unlikely that the over sixty-five people are going to do most of what I have previously listed. Yes, there are those senior daredevils who do extreme sports, but because they are so rare, they rate a half page in the paper.

There are of course some things in the media that are aimed at the senior part of the population—for example incontinence pants, panty liners, haemorrhoid cream, and gadgets for cutting your toenails with extended handles so you don't have to bend over. There are several advertisements for chairs that transport you upstairs, beds that tilt this way and that, and grab rails for the bathroom. There are also handy little sock puller-on gizmos, and don't forget the circular seat for the car so that you can swing your aching limbs free of the car door to plant your feet safely on the ground. Oh joy!

There are a multitude of pages aimed at the over fifty-five group for retirement homes, assisted living, relocatable homes in caravan parks, and innumerable "grey nomad" used vehicles. Does that mean the previous owners did the big trek around Australia and decided once was enough? Does it mean that one of the pair has gone to the great journey in the sky? I don't really care, because it has never been on my wish list.

Cruise holidays adorn the pages where you can travel so cheaply, get fed and watered, and have your bed made every morning. Again, they are usually for two people travelling; if there is only one of you, then you are penalised with a single supplement. I have never been able to figure out why a single supplement is incurred when the accommodation is usually charged at a room cost, presumably for more than one person. If the room charge is two hundred dollars and only one person uses it, shouldn't they charge less? Only half the amount of teabags is used, and if it is single beds, then there is less linen used. Also, if breakfast is included in the tariff, and only one person stays, then the company saves on the cost of breakfast. What exactly is the single supplement for? Does anybody know?

Dating sites are another ageist thing. In some ways this can be good because people generally lie about their age, and from my experience of dating sites, it means that someone looking for a "slick young chick" won't get mixed up with a "grab a granny" web page. It separates the young and clueless from the old and toothless. It is always interesting to go through the postings on these dating sites and read the profiles of those who are listed. The photos of those candidates who wish to deny their age are usually taken from a long way off, a bit grainy and fairly indistinct. You will know they are lying that this photo was taken last year if in the background are the Twin Towers that came down in 2001. Maybe it is a typo, but I suspect not.

I happen to like Bon Jovi, but when I tell people that, they look at me as though I have lost my marbles. Should I just stick to the music of the fifties, or am I allowed to progress a little to the Beatles? I can't see what I look like on the inside, and I do the best I can with the outside, so why shouldn't I go to a rock concert if that is what floats my boat? I have travelled to Melbourne, Perth, and New Zealand to see Bon Jovi, and I wouldn't have missed it for the world. Should I be relegated to opera, which I detest, so that I don't behave disgracefully, yelling out at a rock concert and having no voice the next day? Hell, no—I am not dead yet. I told my daughter that I want "I Did It My Way" played at my funeral, or Bon Jovi's "I'll Live a Lot of Life and I'll Sleep When I'm Dead". See how that perks up the audience, if there is anyone I know who is still alive by the time I go.

I can go and buy the "age-defying mousse", and I pity the salesgirl if she gives me one of those "Why would you bother?" stares. If I want to wear brown eye shadow, or blue or mauve if the mood takes me, then I will. About every two years I go to one of those make-up counters in the department store, with a twenty-something dolly bird in attendance, and get them to advise me on the latest trends. I love the look of despair on their face when they see me heave my cellulite-infested bottom to sit on their lovely, high, cream leather and steel chair. I am sure they would love to have a cupboard to put me in or hide me in some way, but too bad, I am staying here. I usually buy a lipstick just to keep them happy. I then go to the local chemist and replicate the colours, because by the time I put the eye shadow on my eyelids, it usually disappears into the creases anyway, and I only get the minimal effect. But I do try, really I do.

If I want to wear jeans and a baseball cap, then I am damn well going to do it because there is no guidance from the media on what a person over sixty can wear, because obviously they don't care. I just wish I had some of my caftans left from the seventies so that I could hide my not-so-slim figure under it when I am having a fat day. I can wear Jesus sandals if I want, spiky heels, espadrilles laced to my knees, animal-print boots, coloured gumboots, or any other piece of footwear I can find, because there are no rules for my age group. My fashion sense, or lack of it, can be attributed to the eccentricity of my years on earth.

I don't have to have my hair styled in any particular way as dictated by the media, because I don't figure in their articles. I can have my hair grey, but I wouldn't because it is not my favourite colour, though it looks good on some of my friends. I can ask my hairdresser (not stylist, because they charge more) to give me a honey blonde with a few gold streaks and cut it short and spiky. This week I think I will go a bit smoother down the sides and maybe start trying to grow it into a bob. It doesn't really matter what style or colour I have, because I am too old for rules.